Saints and Seasons

BEST REGARDS
Jim McKarns

Saints and Seasons
Reflections for the Liturgical Year

James McKarns

Authors Choice Press
New York Lincoln Shanghai

Saints and Seasons
Reflections for the Liturgical Year

Authors Choice Press
an imprint of iUniverse, Inc.

iUniverse books may be ordered through booksellers or by contacting:

iUniverse
2021 Pine Lake Road, Suite 100
Lincoln, NE 68512
www.iuniverse.com
1-800-Authors (1-800-288-4677)

Originally published by Alba House

ISBN-13: 978-0-595-36013-0
ISBN-10: 0-595-36013-0

Printed in the United States of America

Tell me not, in mournful numbers,
  Life is but an empty dream!
For the soul is dead that slumbers,
  And things are not what they seem.
Life is real! Life is earnest!
  And the grave is not the goal;
Dust thou art, to dust returnest,
  Was not spoken to the soul.

Henry Wadsworth Longfellow:
A Psalm of Life (1839), st. 1,2

TABLE OF CONTENTS

INTRODUCTION

My seminary professor of homiletics once made a statement which I have never forgotten: "Don't go to the pulpit," he said, "just to say something. Go with something to say." We certainly should always have something to say for our subject matter is lofty and dignified. Listeners are present and disposed to hear sacred ideas that will influence their lives.

Homilies should be rated as some of the most outstanding and inspiring talks in the world. Not only do we speak of the most challenging mysteries of life, but we also have such ideal conditions in which to convey our messages. There is an atmosphere of silence, reverence, pleasant surroundings, and respect. The list of advantages goes on like a litany. So if the homily falls short of this exalted image, and surveys say it often does, where is the Achilles' heel?

We always have to ask, "Did the homilist step into the pulpit with something to say?" I personally have a phobia about boring people, wasting their time by sounding empty. If I come to preach a homily which first has not excited me, how in God's name is it going to excite anyone else? I would prefer to preach without a shirt on my back, than to try to preach without a definite message in my heart. Never yet have I met a person who can stand in front of a congregation and successfully "wing it" without previous preparation.

If you, the reader, can find some inspirations in these pages which will excite and entice your heart to pour forth your own lofty wisdom, then you will have accomplished both your mission and mine.

As a directive for daily homilies let me leave you with a bit of advice from Dale Carnegie. "Find a good beginning and a good ending and put them pretty close together."

Saints and Seasons

THE ADVENT SEASON

MONDAY, FIRST WEEK OF ADVENT
Is 2:1-5 or Is 4:2-6 and Mt 8:5-11

The centurion knew that he could achieve immediate results on the strength of his words alone. He also expressed his belief that Jesus, by words alone, could achieve remarkable results as well. Jesus showed amazement at the centurion's statement and praised his faith. In fact, Jesus said that this pagan man had more faith than most in Israel. One word from this Roman centurion was enough to move a hundred men into battle. But just imagine the unrivaled power of God's word! This military leader couched his prayerful request in words of such great confidence that Jesus could hardly refuse him. The Lord has told us to pray with that same faith. In the beginning of this new liturgical year, we ask God to dismiss from our hearts any spiritual sickness we may have. Regardless of how helpless or hopeless a situation may appear, faith teaches us that God's strength is more powerful. Faith, in this instance, brought a healing to one who was not only terribly sick but also paralyzed. The centurion's words are repeated at each Mass before Communion. We may be unworthy but we are not unwelcome.

TUESDAY, FIRST WEEK OF ADVENT
Is 11:1-10 and Lk 10:21-24

As we listen to this reading, we might think it's from a child's story book. The wolf is the guest of the lamb; the calf and lion are browsing together with a little child. Isaiah, the author, is both a dedicated prophet and a superb poet. This is some of his best poetry and it is written not to entertain children, but to teach adults how they should live. It's his visionary prayer for the future, when the Messiah will have arrived. This view of life is a very simple and happy one. Notice these peaceful events will occur on the mountain — a common location for God's presence — rather than down in the dark and cold valley. Can we dream of world peace, believe in it and work for it, as Isaiah did? Jesus, the peacemaker, has already made his entrance into the world — that's to our advantage. We smile at the idea of unfriendly animals snuggling peacefully together. It's the author's way of saying that there is hope for humans. Some animals are natural enemies because of hunger; humans are often mutual enemies because of greed and pride. God's peaceful and holy mountain isn't far away; it's the locality where we live, if we choose to make it such.

WEDNESDAY, FIRST WEEK OF ADVENT
Is 25:6-10 and Mt 15:29-37

As heard yesterday, Isaiah says the Messiah will be found on the holy mountain. There, the best of food and wine will be provided and God will wipe the tears from the peoples' eyes and give them courage. Isaiah is rightfully called the "Prophet of Advent," for his writing is filled with hopeful promises. Seven hundred years later, these messianic prophecies were fulfilled in the person of Jesus. He's on the mountain in today's Gospel. A large crowd of crippled, mute and blind people have gathered around him. The Lord is wiping the tears from their eyes and giving them courage to face the future. We, too, have gathered at the feet of Jesus with our hurts and ills to be healed. Eucharistic food will be provided to bring strength. Our "spiritual loaves" of Eucharistic bread are small but there's enough for all and still have leftovers. Here, Jesus is doing for us what Isaiah foretold the Messiah would do. We will express our faith and make our petitions. Then we will receive the best of food and have the tears wiped from our eyes and courage placed in our hearts — all in the name of Jesus.

THURSDAY, FIRST WEEK OF ADVENT
Is 26:1-6 and Mt 7:21, 24-27

Both readings today emphasize the necessity of a solid basis for one's spiritual life. It must be built on deep faith — symbolized by the image of the rock. In fact, Jesus says that the manner in which we build will determine if we are foolish or wise. Isaiah, too, explicitly proclaims that "the Lord is an eternal rock." All must be based on this eternal rock. Even the lofty city will fall if it becomes too far removed from its foundation. In the Old Testament, the city was always suspect, for it is in the city that people congregate and often plot evil. The Tower of Babel owed its origin to the population of the city where the people plotted with each other to rival God. The tower was a work of extreme pride. If we stay humble and close to the ground, then we won't fall. The old spiritual song, "Rock of Ages," emphasizes the necessity of building our lives of faith on the solid foundation of Jesus. No structure is any stronger than its foundation. "Eternal rock theology" assures us that our structure of faith may be shaken but will not collapse and fall if built on the life and teachings of Jesus.

FRIDAY, FIRST WEEK OF ADVENT
Is 29:17-24 and Mt 9:27-31

During this initial week of Advent, we note that all of the first readings are from Isaiah and five out of six Gospels are from Matthew. With a certain sense of delight, the Church has been demonstrating how the Gospel is the fulfillment of the Isaiah prophecies. Again today our two readings show a clear and definite connection between what Isaiah says the Messiah will do and what Jesus actually accomplishes. Matthew is thereby telling his Jewish readers that Jesus is the Messiah. Isaiah says "on that day," i.e., the day the Messiah arrives, "the eyes of the blind shall see." Then, in the snap of a finger, we bridge 700 years of time and hear Jesus addressing two blind men. They tell Jesus they believe he can cure them and Jesus says because they believe, they will be cured. Although told to keep it quiet, they can't. They must tell everyone. Good news is that way, you can't silence it. We should all appreciate and share the good news of the Savior. Isaiah had a tremendous trust in Jesus long before Jesus was born. Since we have the privilege of looking back at the Lord's life and deeds, our trust and confidence in him should be even deeper and stronger than that of Isaiah.

SATURDAY, FIRST WEEK OF ADVENT
Is 30:19-21, 23-26 and Mt 9:35 - 10:1, 6-8

Isaiah continues to utter promises of hope and joy. He says that God will give the people many basic and needed blessings. Among these are: (1) Removal of sorrows, (2) Plenty of bread and water, (3) Wise teachers, and (4) Benefits for their agricultural way of life. Included in this last category are: rain for the soil, good crops, food for their livestock, clear mountain streams, sunny days and moonlit nights and the healing of bruises. These are the most basic and most precious gifts anyone might want to receive. They are better than the gift of a million dollars. The Church, again, has selected a Gospel passage from Matthew which shows Jesus fulfilling these promises. The Lord sent his apostles forth to bring good news and happy thoughts to people. They were to bestow on them blessings of healing and help. Today, the Church continues to minister to the people of the world. We have the privilege now of being both the recipients and the disbursers of God's wonderful blessings. Think for a moment of some gift you have received and decide how you can freely give it to another.

MONDAY, SECOND WEEK OF ADVENT
Is 35:1-10 and Lk 5:17-26

Jesus had a unique charism about him which inspired other people to accomplish outstanding deeds. He told people to carry their own crosses in imitation of his example. They accepted the challenge and took up those heavy burdens which before had so often weighed them down. The Lord speaks those same words to us. Our crosses may push us into the mud but, with God's assistance, we can still carry them. In this Gospel the paralyzed man is healed and told not only to stand on his feet, but to carry his mat as well. It's an impressive picture of one who had been helplessly carried about on his mat, now being healed and able to carry his mat for himself. His mat is the symbol of his fear, pain and inactivity, but through Jesus he has triumphed over all of them. Our crosses, mats, and whatever else dominates us can be minimized to the point of triviality by the ever present grace of God. The people who met Jesus in faith experienced incredible miracles and so can we. The Lord calls you to leave your mat and do your thing, or as we might say, get off your duff and do your stuff.

TUESDAY, SECOND WEEK OF ADVENT
Is 40:25-31 and Mt 18:12-14

This is a short Gospel that gives a big lift to little people. Jesus addresses his apostles in a very affirming manner — with a question, actually asking their opinions. "What is your thought on this?" The story is told about one stray sheep, which wanders off and gets lost. Neither the hired hand nor the hired shepherd goes to find the sheep but the owner personally does. In his search for the one sheep, he places the other ninety-nine in jeopardy. Is it worth the risk? The owner thinks so. God is symbolized as the owner of the sheep. The stray is not only as important as the others, but as precious as all the others together. The Gospel is wonderfully uplifting to all the little people of the world who feel they don't rate very highly. It's a morale booster to sinful people who are portrayed as the strays who wander off. They are considered much more important in the owner's judgment than they are in their own. If the Father loves the least, then the least should love themselves. The community also must care for one another as the Father cares for each of them.

WEDNESDAY, SECOND WEEK OF ADVENT
Is 40:25-31 and Mt 11:28-30

In the movie, *Chariots of Fire,* the young English runner is preparing for his final race for the Olympic gold medal. Just a few minutes before the starting gun, a friend hands him a note. The runner reads the note, smiles and carries it with him as he races to victory. The words of the note which gave him courage are those read today in the passage of Isaiah. Found in chapter 40, verse 31, the inspiring message is: "They that hope in the Lord will renew their strength, they will soar as with eagles' wings: They will run and not grow weary, walk and not grow faint." These words are very popular today and are often written on T-shirts and sports equipment. They have been set to music and are sung in church. They are read today to give us courage. It was presumed in Isaiah's time, as in ours, that the victory will go to the young and strong. The prophet says that all who hope in the Lord will receive the strength they need to excel. The difficult feat may cause the youth to tire and fall, but the one who draws strength from God will be uplifted and carried to victory by an invisible force, one which has the power of eagle's wings. Hope is help.

THURSDAY, SECOND WEEK OF ADVENT
Is 41:13-20 and Mt 11:11-15

Jesus pays a major compliment to John the Baptizer by saying that John is the greatest person ever born. If John were present on that occasion he must have blushed at the thought, for he was a very humble person. John had publicly stated his personal view that he was of little account when he claimed himself unworthy to unfasten the sandals of Jesus. Yet, it's not what we think of ourselves, whether exalted or humble, that makes us what we really are. As we ponder this thought be ready for what follows. Jesus now says, "The least born into the kingdom of God is greater than John." We are the ones in the Christian kingdom who are referred to as "greater." Do we blush? Do we think it's true? The same rule applies: it's not what we think of ourselves, but what God thinks of us that makes us what we truly are. We should embrace the compliment because Jesus uttered it. The Lord's words should also lift our self image. As followers of Christ, we are people of the kingdom of God and more important than John the Baptizer. Jesus appears to think we have incredible dignity.

FRIDAY, SECOND WEEK OF ADVENT
Is 48:17-19 and Mt 11:16-19

Jesus says that some people are like spoiled children who are never satisfied. If a happy tune is played, they pout, refusing to dance or be glad. If a mournful dirge is sung, they will not cry or wail. Regardless of what others do to please them, there will be some people who will never be satisfied. Those in leadership positions know so well that there will always be someone to find fault with whatever is done. It's good to know that if one did the very opposite, there would be people present who wouldn't agree with that either. Jesus, here, is referring to the scribes and Pharisees who were constantly finding fault with him. When he fasted, they called him strange; when he ate and drank at a party, they called him a drunkard. The quickest way to be very unpopular is to try to please everyone. That is, obviously, impossible to do. We end up pleasing no one and standing for nothing on our own. Someone said the best way to get through life is to give matters your best consideration and then with the mentality of the umpire — call 'em and walk away.

SATURDAY, SECOND WEEK OF ADVENT
Si 48:1-4, 9-11 and Mt 17:10-13

Elijah lived about 850 B.C. He is said to have been transported to heaven in a fiery chariot pulled by horses of fire. Because of his abrupt and dramatic departure, it was believed he would return to earth since he did not die. It became the custom at Jewish tables to set an extra place in case Elijah should return. The similarities between Elijah and Jesus and Elijah and John the Baptizer were numerous. Today's two readings are examples. Some people thought Jesus was Elijah and others said John the Baptizer was. Jezebel sought the life of Elijah just as Herodias had tried to kill John the Baptizer. Elijah's mantle fell upon his successor, Elisha, giving him the double spirit of prophecy. John the Baptizer also prepared both the disciples and the hearts of the people for Jesus, who had more than double his spirit. Elijah, approvingly, stood beside Jesus on Mt. Tabor. Today, these themes and personalities all intertwine in this Advent season. They recall for us our religious traditions and speak of the delicate mysteries of God yet to be unfolded in the future.

MONDAY, THIRD WEEK OF ADVENT
Nb 24:2-7, 15-17 and Mt 21:23-27

The Jewish religious leaders openly confront Jesus in this well-known Gospel passage: "On what authority are you doing these things?" The "things" referred to were the cleansing of the temple, healing the blind and the lame, and teaching. The chief priests were the official teachers of religion and they had not authorized Jesus, so they were challenging him. If Jesus had responded by saying he was operating on God's authority, it would have been too much for them. That would have brought only ridicule and deeper hatred. Jesus, therefore, used the old technique of answering a question with a question. He directs the attention away from himself and re-centers it on John the Baptizer. John was not approved by the Jewish leaders, yet the people believed in him. So Jesus asks his questioners on what authority did John baptize people. The chief priests were in a dilemma — they didn't want to approve of John, nor did they wish to offend the people who believed in him. Their response, "We do not know," was at least a partial admission that it may have been from God. Jesus hopes they might admit that he, too, may be authorized by God. Our faith admits that and celebrates it.

TUESDAY, THIRD WEEK OF ADVENT
Zp 3:1-2, 9-13 and Mt 21:28-32

This Gospel passage teaches us that it's the last decision that makes us what we are, not the first. A person may have led a life of sin and crime and then sincerely reformed. Jesus says the former ways will be forgotten. Shakespeare expressed the same idea when he wrote: "All's well that ends well." This is good news. But remember, the contrary is likewise true. We might have done wonderfully good deeds in our past, but if we are now filled with evil and hate, those past good deeds will not save us. Perhaps as a child we often served Mass and did volunteer work around the church. We might even brag that we attended Catholic school for twelve years, but now we are dishonest, greedy and uncharitable in our dealings with others. We are what we are, not what we were. A field-goal kicker is as popular as his last kick. When he misses the big one in the championship game, no one is going to praise him for some accomplishment five years ago. Jesus tells us that the prostitutes of his day will be held in higher regard than the chief priests because at John's preaching they reformed. This is our season to become what we really want to be.

WEDNESDAY, THIRD WEEK OF ADVENT
Is 45:6-8, 18, 21-25 and Lk 7:18-23

We would think John must have known that Jesus was the one to come and that they were not to expect another. After all, the two of them had established contact and secretly communicated before they were born. However, they were raised about a hundred miles apart and John could now be confused or plagued by doubts. So, from his prison cell, he sent two disciples to meet Jesus and confirm his true identity. Jesus displayed his credentials not by documents or words but by ministering to the poorest of the poor. That is exactly what "the one who is to come" was supposed to be doing. John, at this point in his life, was deliberately beginning to fade from the picture. He was now directing all his followers to Jesus as their new leader. Two of John's disciples got a close-range view of Jesus and witnessed his miracles. They must have been impressed and conveyed their enthusiasm to John and many others. Eventually they would become the leaders of a new Church. We have all come from different backgrounds, have lived in various ways and have met

Jesus in our own unique fashion. How we got here is not too important. It's what we do, now that we are here, that counts. How can I best live my discipleship today?

THURSDAY, THIRD WEEK OF ADVENT
Is 54:1-10 and Lk 7:24-30

In this first reading, God is speaking as a husband to his wife — Zion. Human characteristics are applied to God, who, like the husband, becomes provoked with his wife for a brief time and then tenderly hugs her. These deep emotional feelings are universal and present a fitting metaphor of God's relations with people. We can recognize here a striking similarity to the writings of the prophet Hosea, where the suggestion is made that God was divorcing Israel. There is also a reference to the sixth chapter of Genesis, where God prepares to punish the people with the flood. Then, in chapter eight of Genesis, God vows never to do that again. Can God be perfect and still get angry, repent, "apologize" and promise not to get angry again? Fr. Carroll Stuhlmueller, C.P. calls the teachings of these passages "mysterious theology." Perfection does not mean we must be totally faultless. It does mean we have a perfect ideal and strive for it. When we fall short, we linger there only for a "brief moment," then we immediately try again to pursue our ideal. That's as near to perfection as we are able to come.

FRIDAY, THIRD WEEK OF ADVENT
Is 56:1-3, 6-8 and Jn 5:33-36

In the ancient pagan world, a mountain was often regarded as the proper place to worship. It was thought that the gods dwelt there or could best be contacted on one of the "high places." Isaiah, here, speaks of a holy mountain, where the Messiah will establish a house of prayer. The people will offer sacred worship to the one true God. An altar shall adorn the house of prayer where sacrifices will be offered. People will climb the mountain to pray and all will be equal. No one shall be considered a foreigner. It shall be a sacred place. The temple was built in the mountain city of Jerusalem and the house of prayer was used for many centuries. It was there Jesus drove out the money changers for making it more a place of business than a house of prayer. Today, we are in our house of prayer, about our altar, offering our sacrifice. We remember and celebrate our salvation accomplished on another mountain — Calvary. Jesus, the Messiah, has fulfilled the prophecies of Isaiah and we now gather to fulfill the wishes of the Messiah. Here, we worship in spirit and truth.

DECEMBER 17
Gn 49:2, 8-10 and Mt 1:1-17

The genealogy of Jesus is read today from the Gospel of St. Matthew. Some of the names are more familiar to us than others, but they all form a vital link between the earthly ancestors of Jesus. They are traced to the time of Abraham, the father of the Hebrew people. Through this genealogy, the faith of Abraham is personified and manifested in the Messiah. Many people in modern times like to investigate their family trees. Some seek out past information from a sense of curiosity or sentimentality, looking for some famous ancestor. Others search into the past to verify rights of inheritance of money or property. After the death of Howard Hughes, at least 100 "cousins," surfaced to share in the wealth. Some regret their efforts when it's pointed out they must pay the back taxes. We also have a spiritual blood line which can be traced back to Jesus. Our religious family tree is the cross. There, we discover the divinity and royalty of our famous ancestor and savior. We are proud and uplifted by our spiritual genealogy.

DECEMBER 18
Jr 23:5-8 and Mt 1:18-24

Dream interpretation continues to find practitioners of greater or lesser credibility. The old theory that a dream occurs only because we are uncomfortable and not resting well has, for the most part, been abandoned. It is said the part of the brain that triggers the dream is the cortex — the oldest area. That is supposed to explain why so many dreams take us back to childhood happenings and situations. The meanings of dreams should not be totally dismissed as nonsense. There may be some hidden religious message there for us. Matthew says Joseph had a directive dream as he pondered the question of his marriage to Mary. An angel spoke to him and relayed valuable information. It was the dream which confirmed his decision to proceed with the wedding. Numerous people of the Bible have had dreams and used them to direct their future courses of action. We may not have angels speaking to us at night, but everyone should have some dreams which he or she would like to see fulfilled. For us a "dreaming time" can mean thinking, planning and praying about what we would like to do. We, too, trust in God's help and then set out to make our dream come true.

DECEMBER 19
Jg 13:2-7, 24-25 and Lk 1:5-25

In ancient times the conception and birth of a child was much more mystery-filled than today. It bespoke the presence of God in the lives of the parents. The presence of sterility was regarded as a divine disfavor. If a child was conceived in very unlikely circumstances, that was a clear sign of God's benign intervention. The readings today show two very clear cases of God's presence in peoples' lives. Hannah is childless and in answer to her prayer and vow to dedicate her child to Yahweh, she gives birth to Samson. The child was born with his religious mission already determined. Elizabeth is sterile and very advanced in age. An angel appears to her husband and promises a child, which eventually is born. Because of circumstances like these, there is no doubt that God will be with this baby boy. These two scriptural stories are read during the Advent season to help prepare us for the biggest surprise of all. Mary has conceived her child in a most unusual manner. Soon, we will know that God is not only with the child, but the child is God incarnate.

DECEMBER 20
Is 7:10-14 and Lk 1:26-38

When we hear a passage of Scripture which is very familiar, we can easily overlook some of its impact, thinking we have heard it all before. The Gospel reading today is certainly well-known and often heard by us. Have you ever considered it from the point of view of Jesus fulfilling what was predicted about him? We can note at least five points where predictions about him have been fulfilled. (1) Mary was to give the child the name "Jesus." The name was given even before he was conceived by his mother. (2) It was said "great will be his dignity." Today we offer no higher dignity to anyone than we give to Jesus. (3) He would be "called Son of the Most High." Christians have always taught and believed that Jesus is the Son of the Most High God. (4) He would be given "the throne of David." The Lord embodies all the royalty of David and much more. (5) It is said "his reign will be without end." David was king for forty years; Jesus reigns forever. This passage is a bold statement about the future. Christmas is the annual birthday celebration of the one who is no ordinary child.

DECEMBER 21
Sg 2:8-14 and Lk 1:39-45

Both the Song of Solomon and the Gospel of Luke dance and leap with the spiritual joy of new beginnings. A lover is on his way to his beloved. The two can hardly wait to meet and start their new life together. It's the springtime of the year and the springtime of their lives. They, definitely, are in love. This passage is probably so often read and quoted because it gives hope not only to face tomorrow but to find there a joyful fulfillment. In the Gospel, the unborn babies — John and Jesus, are restless with excitement. They seem eager to be born, to develop, and to begin their respective missions. Already in their mothers' wombs they are communicating with each other. Each day we are provided with a number of favorable opportunities to find similar excitement and joy. The memories of the past may be very good, but trust in God and hope in life itself can always entice us into the fresh new dreams of future opportunities. With the coming of Christmas, we can, like a child, leap and dance with joy and excitement. We have the opportunity to be as jubilant as we make up our minds to be.

DECEMBER 22
1 S 1:24-28 and Lk 1:46-56

This is Mary's longest recorded prayer. It was inspired by God, voiced in the presence of Elizabeth, and has been repeated a billion times. Known simply as the Magnificat, from its first word in the Latin translation, it is based on the prayer of Hannah for her son Samson (1 S 2:1-10). That passage is presented in today's liturgy as the responsorial psalm. The striking parallels are obvious. Mary's thoughts are both clear and lofty. She asks for nothing and expresses no guilt or sorrow for sin. Her exalted thoughts are poured out in the highest spirit of praise and thanksgiving. Mary has a very wholesome and healthy concept of God. Especially, she says, "I find joy in God my Savior." If we want to imitate the unique spirituality of Mary, we will sincerely attempt to dismiss debilitating fears from our lives and think of God with exultant joy. The powerful theme of thanksgiving also threads its way through this beautiful prayer of Mary. It should, likewise, be the fabric of our lives. Perhaps, too often we see only the fearful God of punishment. Mary encourages us to discover the loving God of joy.

DECEMBER 23
Ml 3:1-4, 23-34 and Lk 1:57-66

If the relatives and neighbors of Elizabeth would have had their way, today, we would be referring to Zechariah the Baptizer. We witness here the strong family and community influence in Elizabeth's life, from the fact the relatives and neighbors tried to name her child. When Elizabeth protests, "No, he is to be called John," they still object by pointing out in a protesting manner that she is breaking tradition. "None of your relatives has this name." They try to override her objections by appealing to the child's father. They must think that, surely, the father would be very happy to have the child named after him. When he, too, stated categorically, "His name is John," their insistence was turned into complying wonderment. Tradition has its value but sometimes even sacred traditions and customs must be set aside in favor of something which is new. Because some practice is traditional, it doesn't have to be perpetual. Traditions can come to fulfillment and, then, God breaks into the cycle, with a better idea and steers the old tradition in a new direction. Take Christmas for example.

DECEMBER 24
2 S 7:1-5. 8-11. 16 and Lk 1:67-79

The liturgy of the Church, with this Mass, has now set the stage for the birth of Jesus. The Lord has been predicted through the various personalities of the Hebrew Scriptures. This has transpired over many centuries. The high quality of the people involved and the extreme length of time, augment the importance of the long awaited one. Excitement is in the air and at the doorstep. Baby John is born and his father sings his praises. He is unique, precious, holy and, yet, he is not the expected one — only the messenger. So if little six-month-old John is blessed, how much more sacred will be the long awaited Messiah whom he will introduce! Later, John would say he was not even worthy to loosen the sandal straps of Jesus. Leaving these lofty thoughts lingering in our minds, the liturgy rests its case. The next logical step will be to welcome Jesus to our world and into our lives. It's just one tiny step away now. Thus it is each year, the liturgy brings us to the annual celebration of the birth of Jesus. God visits us "who sit in darkness . . . to guide our feet into the way of peace."

THE CHRISTMAS SEASON

DECEMBER 26 - FEAST OF ST. STEPHEN, FIRST MARTYR
Ac 6:8-10, 7:54-59 and Mt 10:17-22

Stephen, the deacon, died not only with the spirit of Jesus in his heart but with the words of Jesus on his tongue. Stephen had molded his spiritual life into a fine imitation of his Lord and Savior. Like Jesus, he is said to have been "filled with grace and power, one who worked great wonders and signs among the people." None of his adversaries were a match for his wisdom. Luke says Stephen had a vision of Jesus in the sky just before he was dragged out of the city and stoned to death. His final words sound like an echo from Calvary, "Lord Jesus, receive my spirit." Then, falling to his knees, he adds, "Lord, do not hold this sin against them." In the heroic style of the Savior, Stephen thus became the first Christian martyr. The charge against him was that he was "teaching disobedience to the customs and rules of Moses." You might want to read his remarkable homily, just before he died, recorded in chapter 7 of the Acts. St. Stephen's Day is always observed on December 26.

DECEMBER 27 - FEAST OF ST. JOHN, APOSTLE AND EVANGELIST
1 Jn 1:1-4 and Jn 20:2-8

John carries the impressive dual title of apostle and evangelist. This first reading, whether written by the apostle himself or one fully imbued with his spirit, contains a tremendous amount of spiritual enthusiasm. John wants nobody to doubt the facts about Jesus or even to hint that the apostles could have been mistaken about the true identity of the Lord. You catch in this passage the forceful sincerity of a person possessed to tell the truth to convince all who heard. "We proclaim to you," he says, "what we have heard . . . have seen . . . have looked upon and our hands have touched." The writer has a happy grasp of eternal life and wants to share it with all others. John is often called the Son of Zebedee and brother of James to distinguish him from John the Baptizer. He was called to the ministry from his father's fishing boat to become not only one of the Twelve, but one of the privileged Three. He, along with Peter and James, witnessed many events the others did not see, notably the contrasting highs and lows of the Transfiguration and the Agony in the Garden. John was convinced that Jesus loved him intently, almost to the point of bragging about his relationship with the Lord. We have every reason to believe that God loves us just as much. Maybe we, like John, should be more enthusiastic.

DECEMBER 28 - FEAST OF THE HOLY INNOCENTS, MARTYRS
1 Jn 1:5 - 2:2 and Mt 2:13-18

This passage from Matthew giving Joseph instructions for the flight into Egypt follows the same sequence as those directions for accepting Mary as his wife. (1) An angel appears suddenly in a dream. (2) A command is issued and a reason for it. (3) Joseph is resolved to carry it out. (4) There is a quotation from the Hebrew Scriptures showing how this fulfills a prophecy. Egypt was regarded as a common place of refuge for Jews who were being persecuted at that time. It was therefore a logical destination for the Holy Family. They imitate their ancient ancestors who also left Israel for Egypt, stayed for awhile and returned home. It is biblically appropriate that a bit of Egyptian culture should touch the life of Jesus. There is some question about the total credibility of the killing of the innocent children. No other mention is made about this manner of eliminating a future rival from the throne. Josephus, the historian does note some of the gruesome deeds done by Herod but not this one. Today's liturgy

commemorates all the innocent people who die because of the
cruelty of others. It's sad to realize that even the baby Jesus was
not exempt from jealous hatred.

DECEMBER 29
1 Jn 2:3-11 and Lk 2:22-35

Simeon came to the temple each day for many years expecting someday to see the Messiah. This is the day. Simeon, enlightened by the Holy Spirit, instantly recognizes Jesus. Taking the
baby in his outstretched arms, he says now he can die in peace for
he has seen the Lord — his light and glory. The temple is the
bonding place between Judaism and Christianity and the first
public pronouncement of coming salvation is now taking place
within its precincts. Simeon and Anna represent two devout
religious Jews who are not threatened by the coming fulfillment of
Judaism in Christianity. Being guided by the Spirit means that
they constantly relied on God for direction in their lives. Imagine
the peaceful transition which would have occurred if all the Jews
had been as open and accepting of Jesus. Simeon realizes most
will not be as accepting, thus he confidently predicts the troubles
ahead for Jesus and his parents. He foresees that the Pharisees
will offer Jesus nothing but opposition and persecution. Are we
looking for Jesus today? Faith can enable us to find our Lord and
hold him near our hearts, just as Simeon did.

DECEMBER 30
1 Jn 2:12-17 and Lk 2:36-40

Anna was eighty-four years old. Everyone around the temple knew her since she was there everyday until closing time.
She, as a young lady, had lived with her husband for only seven
years before he died. Since then she remained a widow and found

fulfillment in her religion. In the temple she fasted and prayed
hoping to see the Messiah. It was there she finally discovered the
one who would make her happy forever. Luke says of Anna, "she
had seen many days," but this day was the best. After the visit to
the temple, the parents returned home with the baby Jesus and
he grew taller, stronger and more grace-filled. Jesus was, in his
own person, the new Temple being shaped into place. Eventually, the Lord would develop to such a point that he would
supercede the Jewish temple. Anna and Simeon are two of the
original Christian-Jews. They were able to see the natural connection between Jesus and Judaism. If we are determined to find
Jesus and make the effort necessary, we too will be successful.
Jesus said, "Seek and you will find."

DECEMBER 31
1 Jn 2:18-21 and Jn 1:1-18

Here we have a remarkable passage of Scripture. It used to
be read at the conclusion of every Mass. The words speak of the
long journey of God's Son from the deep and mysterious recesses
of eternity into the material realities of earthly time and space.
When we think of the past history leading up to the visible
appearance of Jesus, we normally would turn to the genealogies
found in both Matthew and Luke. Here, however, we have a third
genealogy — a spiritual one. It totally dwarfs the other two. Just
imagine how long ago it was when only God existed and there was
nothing else. God was like a light shining in the lonely darkness.
That light could not be conquered by the pervading gloom. Indeed, from that powerful and loving light, there came all that is.
God reveals himself through creation and then the most fantastic
manifestation of all occurs when human flesh is wrapped about the
spirit of God. Now for the first time God is truly visible to human
eyes in the person of Jesus. The song might say it best: "Mine
eyes have seen the glory of the coming of the Lord."

JANUARY 2
1 Jn 2:22-28 and Jn 1:19-28

When the Jews asked John the Baptizer, "Who are you?" he replied by saying who he wasn't. "I'm not the Messiah," he answered. Knowing who we are not helps us know who we are. There's a story told about a man going to make a five-day retreat. When he checked in on Sunday evening the receptionist asked what he hoped to obtain from the coming retreat. "I don't expect to discover profound theological truths," he said. "I just want the answer to a couple of simple questions. I want to know, first, who is God, and secondly, who am I." When leaving on Friday afternoon, the receptionist bade the man good-bye and inquired if he had found the answers to his two questions. "Oh yes," he replied, "I now understand that Jesus is God and I'm not." John is such an outstanding saint because he knew he was not God, nor the Messiah, nor Elijah, nor one of the ancient prophets. He was bigger than life in the view of others, but in his own estimation he was simply another of God's friends - only a voice and a very humble one. Being honest to ourselves makes us honest to God.

JANUARY 3
1 Jn 2:29 - 3:6 and Jn 1:29-34

John loves to designate the followers of Jesus simply as the "Children of God." Imagine, if all Christians today would be given the official title of "Children of God." Our many different denominations and titles divide us from each other. It is very encouraging to remember that our various denominations of Protestant, Orthodox and Catholic are all Christian. We are Christians and therefore to be known as "Children of God." John is reflecting the teachings of Jesus when he says that we are called to be members of one family. Jesus taught the Lord's Prayer, which clearly implies that we are one family because we have one Heavenly Father. The plural is emphasized over the singular. It's "*Our* Father . . . give *us* . . . *Our* daily bread . . . lead *us* . . . deliver *us* . . ." We are to think as one family. There is the heavenly Father and we are the children. The passage we heard in today's first reading you may have recognized because it is often read on the occasion of funerals. What we will later become "has not yet come to light." The more we can trust God with childlike faith, the more we are acting as true children of God.

JANUARY 4
1 Jn 3:7-10 and Jn 1:35-42

The first chapter of John's Gospel contains fifty-one verses. The first eighteen verses comprise the spiritual genealogy of Jesus — as discussed two days ago. The remaining thirty-three verses are presented in the framework of each day of the week. This section is a type of parallel to the original creation story in Genesis where something new and different happened on each of the seven days. John begins his Gospel showing that a new creation is developing in Jesus which will supercede the original one that was flawed by the sin of Adam and Eve. Here, in the seven-day framework of the New Testament, various individuals testify to the true identity of Jesus as the saving Messiah. Today's reading picks up the theme on the third day at 4:00 p.m. John tells his disciples to abandon him and follow Jesus for he is the "Lamb of God." On the following days, Philip will testify to Jesus, then Nathaniel, and finally Jesus will work the Cana miracle on the seventh day. Spirituality calls us to continually seek and accept the better way as we move from the Alpha to the Omega of our earthly existence.

JANUARY 5
1 Jn 3:11-21 and Jn 1:43-51

The themes of new beginnings continues to surface in our daily readings. This is fitting in conjunction with the first days of the new year. The New Testament is shown to be superior to the Old, where Cain killed his brother. Here again it is stated how we are to love our brothers and sisters. Strong language is used to make this point of the necessity of loving others. "The one who does not love is among the living-dead. Anyone who hates his brother and sister is a murderer and you know that eternal life abides in no murderer's heart." The tremendous struggle continues between good and evil and life and death. We are to be the exact opposite of Cain and protect the lives of our brothers and sisters even by laying down our own lives. That is the ultimate test of genuine love. True Christian love then is to be seen in actions not just heard in words. The "new way" of Christianity teaches a love which is total and life demanding. Do we have that high a calibre of genuine love for others? If so, we are children of God. If not, we have yet to grasp and live the Christian message to the full.

JANUARY 6
1 Jn 5:5-13 and Mk 1:7-11

From the pen of Mark, we hear the words and see the deeds of John the Baptizer. The self-effacing prophet rates himself unworthy to be even a servant of Jesus. He says, "I am not fit to stoop and untie his sandal straps." John, most likely, had a good image of himself per se, for he preached to others about reforming their lives. In the presence of Jesus, however, he saw himself in a diminishing role for Jesus was to be exalted. He would be the last person on earth to become a rival for the Lord. John's adulation for Jesus was as a starry-eyed fan in the presence of a famous sport's figure. In a different setting, he might have said, he was over-awed to carry his bat or glove or touch his shoes. We all would do well to renew our sense of awe and respect for the Lord. The old Scripture saying that the fear of the Lord is the beginning of wisdom should be remembered. The term fear in that text means, respect or reverence. Jesus is the beloved of the Father and God's favor does rest on him. That, alone, makes Jesus deserving of all our love and reverential respect. How can we show that today?

JANUARY 7
1 Jn 5:14-21 and Jn 2:1-12

We noted several days ago that John is presenting here a new version of the Genesis creation story. This one is centered about Jesus. He has now arrived on the seventh day. The previous six days have been leading to this climax. John the Baptizer has testified to the fact that Jesus is the one who was to come, as have some of his disciples. Now Jesus substantiates their confidence in him and displays his authenticity. Thus, the water of the Old Testament now becomes the wine of the New. This is the first miracle which Jesus performs and one which speaks of the generosity of God. The grace Jesus has provided for us is more than enough — just like the wine. It is emphatically pointed out how much better the second wine is compared to the first. John is saying that the teachings of our Lord far surpass in depth and scope anything which has been produced in prior ages. God is now revealing himself through his Messiah and proclaiming an unambiguous truth — he makes neither cheap wine nor cheap people. The wine as a symbol of redemptive grace is not only of high quality but there is more than enough for everyone. All is set in the framework of a wedding, showing that it is through love we find God, each other, and ultimate salvation.

MONDAY AFTER EPIPHANY
1 Jn 3:22 - 4:6 and Mt 4:12-17, 23-25

John the Baptizer had a favorite theme he often preached, "Reform your lives! The kingdom of heaven is at hand." Matthew tells us that when John was arrested, Jesus began to preach that very same message since John had been silenced. Jesus and John, in many ways, worked as a team and promoted a unified mission. When John was arrested, Jesus did not try to obtain his release. Thus, the circumstances were unfolding as Scripture had foretold and God had planned. Our lives are to be continual efforts to reform and, in doing so, we will encounter a healthy mixture of favorable and unfavorable events. This message is basic to the followers of Jesus today and the Church continues to proclaim it. The call to reform doesn't imply we are terrible sinners. Saints, too, are called to an ongoing reform of their lives. Reform means literally to "form again." We are to continually reshape our spiritual lives into what they ought to be. When we reform anything, we try to make it better and renew it. In what ways could we better follow the advice of John the Baptizer and Jesus by improving the ways in which we are now living?

TUESDAY AFTER EPIPHANY
1 Jn 4:7-10 and Mk 6:34-44

John writes a key sentence in this passage, "The person without love," he says, "has known nothing of God." One may know much about love and still understand little about God. We can't, however, know God and yet be ignorant about the meaning of love. Love, like God, is strong, sensitive and enduring. It's also forgiving. God is love and, as love itself, God is continually producing good results like feeding the crowd in this Gospel passage. Love has a unique way of multiplying the best in every situation. So it happens that a little bread and a few fish plus the love of God, produces fantastic results. The formula for the multiplication of the loaves and the fishes is: $5 + 2 +$ God's blessings $= 5,000$ plus. Obviously, the main elements are not the loaves and fishes. The miracle is the multiplication of divine love. Now, we have a little bread and wine today. And, over it, we ask God's blessing. The bread becomes our spiritual food and we are strengthened in the love of God which has been multiplied on the altar and within each person's faith-filled heart.

WEDNESDAY AFTER EPIPHANY
1 Jn 4:11-18 and Mk 6:45-52

This first reading from John explains the marvelous effects of God's enduring love. Within the person who is filled with love, there is no room for fear. John succinctly says that "perfect love casts out all fear." With that in mind, the Gospel makes a clear commentary on the lack of genuine love to be found in the hearts of the apostles. They need to develop a much deeper love if they ever hope to be without fear. Their fears are very evident in this incident where Jesus comes to them walking on the water. First, they're afraid of the storm. Then, Mark says, the high winds frighten them. Finally, the entire group is terrified by Jesus himself. In the early morning darkness, they mistake him for a ghost. In essence, Jesus was both saying and demonstrating that they had a long way to go in order to achieve that perfect love which casts out all fear. If the fear of God is the beginning of wisdom, then complete wisdom is found in the love of God. When our love of God is complete then all fear will have disappeared. Can I live this day with so much love of God that my fears will, at least temporarily disappear?

THURSDAY AFTER EPIPHANY
1 Jn 4:19 - 5:4 and Lk 4:14-22

Several boys in the third grade were continually fighting on the playground. The teacher talked to the whole class about love and forgiveness and especially directed her remarks to Joey and Billy, two of the worst offenders. Several days later, while going through Billy's papers, the teacher found this little note which Joey had written to his "partner in crime" following her talk. "Dear Billy, I hate you. Love, Joey." The lives of children and adults are a strange mixture of love and hate. A loving person can often feel anger, but will soon overcome it and forgive the offense, ready to begin again. John tells us that God has loved us first. This applies not only to the past but also when we sin in the present. God is the first to love and to take steps toward reconciliation. Most likely we are forgiven before we ever ask. This is the way we should behave towards others. I complain because someone will not speak to me, and I refuse to speak to that individual until he or she speaks first. How often we argue about who started a dispute and who should make the initial move to forgive. To forgive first is often interpreted as an admission of guilt and a sign of weakness. John says that the opposite is true. When we make the first move, we are the ones who are strong for we are imitating the conduct of God.

FRIDAY AFTER EPIPHANY
1 Jn 5:5-13 and Lk 5:12-16

This Gospel miracle was accomplished by Jesus directly and without delay. There were no questions on the part of Jesus about the person's state of mind. The reason was because the petitioner had come with an obvious abundance of faith. The request was not, "Cure me if you can," but, "If you will to do so, you can cure me." The man making the request was "full of leprosy," but he was likewise filled with faith. He never doubted whether or not Jesus could heal him. He knew he could. It was only a question of "if he willed to do so." Jesus quickly rewarded this man's deep faith with the response, "I do will it. Be cured." This type of profound faith in Jesus gets an immediate and powerful response from the Lord. It causes John to say in the first reading that we can conquer the world if we believe in Jesus as the Son of God. He even goes so far as to say, "Whoever possesses the Son (through faith) possesses life." It would be beneficial for us to seriously consider how our lives could improve with a deeper and more loving trust in God. Jesus praises all those who have faith in him and gives us every reason imaginable why we ought to have it.

SATURDAY AFTER EPIPHANY
1 Jn 5:14-21 and Jn 3:22-30

Dr. Brackett was a physician who lived, served, and died in one small town. He could have moved to a bigger and better practice, but he stayed in the same small town where he cared for the poor. He often charged them practically nothing for his medical ministry. His office was located on Main Street above a clothing store. A large brass plate was attached to the street-level door indicating that his office was on the second floor. It read: "Dr. Brackett, Office Upstairs." When the beloved old doctor died, someone removed the sign form the door and placed it on his grave, indicating the new location of the office of this good man. John the Baptizer, like Dr. Brackett, aspired only to the office of being of service to others. He did not want or need to be Number One. In relation to Jesus, John the Baptizer was highly honored to be the proverbial "best man." We may not think of it as a high calling or any kind of challenge to be of service to others, but that's the route to holiness which millions have traveled. Perfection begins by being a faithful servant. Only then are we invited by the Master to come up higher.

THE LENTEN SEASON

ASH WEDNESDAY
Jl 2:12-18 and Mt 6:1-6, 16-18

This passage from the Prophet Joel, which has become so identified with the Ash Wednesday liturgy, was written originally in response to an invasion of locusts. They were eating the crops and seriously causing panic among the people who feared immediate hunger and possible starvation. The whole country, therefore, was called upon to repent and beg God to destroy the locusts, save the crops, and spare the people from suffering. The text is easily applicable to the beginning of the Lenten season. Lent, too, is a universal call to all the people to reform, repent, and renew their lives by resolving to live more in keeping with the teachings of the Gospel. Lent always comes during the springtime of the year in the Northern Hemisphere, making it a season of optimism and new hope. The ancient practices of prayer, fasting, and almsgiving are recommended for our personal and community improvement. Beyond these traditional practices, many other devotions and spiritual projects can be pursued. We might resolve to forgive an enemy, assist an unfortunate person, or meditate on the six powerful themes for the Sundays of the season. One basic Lenten duty is to concentrate on God's goodness more than on our own sinfulness and thus expand the narrow bounds of our thinking.

THURSDAY AFTER ASH WEDNESDAY
Dt 30:15-20 and Lk 9:22-25

All three synoptic evangelists record in their Gospels the passage read at today's liturgy. The three accounts are very similar, but Luke adds an additional thought about carrying one's cross. Where Matthew and Mark say we should carry our crosses, Luke adds the words, "each day." We could take up our crosses periodically and still say we are following Jesus' command. Luke, however, makes sure we understand that this is something which is to be done on a daily basis. Perhaps the Church chose Luke's Gospel today, rather than one of the others, to emphasize this extended thought of daily commitment. The exhortation is especially meaningful on this second day of Lent. We can easily be inspired about this penitential season on Ash Wednesday, but the real test begins now, on the day after. Our resolutions and programs for spiritual improvement must be followed on a regular, daily basis if we hope to achieve any success. Those who are faithful daily, and dependable in their prayers and good deeds, will be the ones who are recognized as the true disciples of Jesus.

FRIDAY AFTER ASH WEDNESDAY
Is 58:1-9 and Mt 9:14-15

Both the Hebrew prophet, Isaiah, and Jesus himself endorse the spiritual value of fasting. A clear warning, though, is given in today's liturgical readings that fasting is not to be done just for the sake of saying that you've done it. The purpose of fasting is for achieving a certain goal — an improvement in our interior life. We have to fulfill our basic duties to God before fasting will do any good. To fast and yet neglect these more fundamental responsibilities would be to fast in vain. First of all we must have faith in our hearts. Then we must perform works of mercy and practice justice in our dealings with our neighbors. And all of these are to be done in an overall spirit of Christian love. This mode of spiritual thinking and decent living must be present first. Otherwise, everything else we do of a religious nature will be of little account. Are we needlessly oppressing others by our words, habits or suspicions? If we want God to smile upon us, we must first release our captives. Then we will be ready to move on to other more advanced levels of spirituality. Perhaps at this point we find ourselves unable to fast in a way which is truly pleasing to God. If that is the case, Lent is an excellent time to reform. It is a season of many graces.

SATURDAY AFTER ASH WEDNESDAY
Is 58:9-14 and Lk 5:27-32

Luke informs us that Levi was sitting at the tax collector's post when Jesus called him to discipleship. He followed and eventually became one of the twelve apostles. But who in the world is Levi? Have we ever met him before? In relating this same incident, Mark tells us that Levi is the son of Alpheus. Still not much help in identifying him. Matthew, too, tells this story. And it is he who solves the mystery, for he is the one known as Levi. It is possible that Levi was his family name and thus both Mark and Luke address him formally and correctly. The name Levi, often associated with money and business, is the name of the head of one of the twelve patriarchal tribes of Israel from whom the Levites take their name. After leaving his tax collecting post and beginning a new life, he chose to be called by his first name, Matthew. It means "gift of God." In his new life he always uses his new name in describing events in which he was personally involved. A parallel in reverse is to be found in the case of Nathaniel Bartholomew, who is better known by his last name than his first. A new way of life and a new name are exciting possibilities for us to consider during this sacred season of Lent. What does my name mean to me and to others who know me? There are certain aspects of my life which I could change for the better. When I achieve those objectives, my image will be enriched and my name will have a new meaning.

MONDAY OF THE FIRST WEEK OF LENT
Lv 19:1-2, 11-18 and Mt 25:31-46

In our reading of Leviticus, we are presented with a restatement of the Old Testament commandments. They explain the minimum expected of us as believers, telling us what we should and should not do as we act and interact with God and others. Notice that the emphasis in the Ten Commandments is on the external and the tone is basically negative. By contrast, the Gospel of Matthew presents the Works of Mercy. These have become the new commandments for the followers of Jesus. The setting of this Gospel is the judgment scene at the end of time. Salvation is being determined here, not according to the way we have lived the Ten Commandments, but on how well we have observed the Works of Mercy. We may think of the sins we have committed and worry about how they've separated us from God. Yet it is very likely that the ones with which we are most concerned are not listed as the most serious on the Lord's "worry list." Salvation here is equated not to the traditional Ten Commandments but to how well we have served the less fortunate individuals in our midst. We may recite long litanies, practice the ancient or most modern devotions, meditate on the deepest theological insights of the day, but this Gospel says that the surest and most direct road to salvation is to be found in performing the Works of Mercy.

TUESDAY OF THE FIRST WEEK OF LENT
Is 55:10-11 and Mt 6:7-15

Isaiah here gives us a very thoughtful reflection on the meaning of the word of God. The word of God is more than a sound or a combination of sounds used to express an idea. Sounds are inanimate and, once spoken, they forever disappear. The

word of God is much more than that. It's more like a material
object, in the nature of a missile on a mission. Its objective is to
make contact with our ears and penetrate our minds. There it
releases its message of hope and joy and we are changed and
converted to accomplish what the word has taught. Isaiah tells us
that the word of God is as the rain and snow which come down
from the sky. They come with the purpose of watering the earth,
making it fertile and fruitful. The earth's mission is to produce
something — first a tender shoot from the seed and then the grain
for bread. The word does not return to God unless its mission is
accomplished. Every sound from Scripture is like a drop of rain or
a ray of sunshine. Attend carefully to it, for the payload that it
brings to you is literally heaven-sent. Accept that truth into your
lives and God will not have spoken in vain.

WEDNESDAY OF THE FIRST WEEK OF LENT
Jon 3:1-10 and Lk 11:29-32

Jesus, as a young Jewish boy, would have read and studied
the Old Testament in preparation for his Bar Mitzvah. He undoubtedly found many heroes and heroines within those sacred
pages. One of his heroes would have been the prophet Jonah.
Jesus spoke about Jonah on at least two occasions, both of which
are recorded in Scripture. Once he described how the people of
Nineveh repented when Jonah preached to them. That incident is
recorded in both readings of this liturgy. On another occasion,
Jesus predicted that he would be in the tomb for three days,
comparing himself during this ordeal to Jonah's being in the belly
of the fish for three days. Solomon was another hero of Jesus. He
admired his wisdom. Solomon is also mentioned in our Gospel
today. Heroes though they are, Jesus can unblushingly proclaim
that he surpasses the best of them: "You have a greater than
Jonah . . . than Solomon here." We have the luxury of having

Jesus as our hero. We can study his life, read his words, and accept his loving grace. Trying to think and live as Jesus did should not be considered drudgery or painful. Most find it exciting trying to imitate their heroes.

THURSDAY OF THE FIRST WEEK OF LENT
Est C 12:14-16, 23-25 and Mt 7:7-12

Jesus possessed a unique talent for simplifying religious subjects. His response about prayers being answered is a good example. Our ancestors, like ourselves, must have found it very confusing. Today's Gospel could have easily been inspired by the question, "How do I get my prayers answered?" The Lord states simply, "Ask, and you will receive." Do we believe that it's that simple? If Jesus said it, we should believe it. You might remember the many things you have asked for and never received. Notice, though, that Jesus doesn't tell us that we will receive what we ask for. Also, if we do receive it, he does not promise that it will come immediately. Whenever we ask, we do receive something. The asking itself is an expression of faith. The answer given brings us joy. The answer not given brings us humility. All three are precious gifts. One or more of them is always there in the asking, just as Jesus said. Seeking to find and knocking to open are but other ways to express the same idea. We should pray often, for God cannot answer a prayer which has not been prayed. When we pray as Jesus did, "Thy will, not mine, be done," and mean it, we will always be at peace with the answer we receive.

FRIDAY OF THE FIRST WEEK OF LENT
Ezk 18:21-28 and Mt 5:20-26

Ezekiel is not read very often in the liturgy but we have a passage from his writings in today's first reading. The content expressed here can cause us to reevaluate some common current attitudes. We've all heard people make statements such as, "I don't go to church too much now, but when I was a kid I'd go every Sunday and serve Mass, attend novenas and even helped clean the pews." The inference is that past good deeds will compensate for present neglect. Ezekiel assures us that this is not the case. We can't coast through life on our past spiritual achievements. In fact, the prophet tells us, the very opposite is true. We might have been very evil and neglectful in the past, but now that we've reformed and are doing much better, we will find that the past will be forgotten by God. The fear is always that virtuous people will turn to evil; the joy is that sinners can become saints. We will all be what we choose to be. I must remember today that I am not the person that I used to be. I am the person I am.

SATURDAY OF THE FIRST WEEK OF LENT
Dt 26:16-19 and Mt 5:43-48

Jesus is a very demanding person and he knows it. Here he restates the old law with the implication that it wasn't very difficult to observe. After all, to "love your countryman but hate your enemy" is something we would naturally do. Those who originally heard him preaching this message would probably have been very happy had he stopped with that quotation. They could have all gone home peacefully, feeling very self-righteous. But the Lord didn't stop. He gave a new commandment — one which was much more demanding. In fact, it is so demanding that it seems almost contradictory. "Love your enemies, pray for your persecutors!" How can we love our enemies, those who hate us? Or why should we love them? If we love our enemies, wouldn't that mean that they would cease being our enemies? Hating them, we can understand. But loving them? It's the Lord's way of

saying, "Don't have enemies, at least from your point of view."
Love them right out of existence by making them your friends.
Now that is certainly a lofty ideal! This is one of the most difficult
commandments we have. How we fare with this one will say
much about our real commitment to the ways of Jesus.

MONDAY OF THE SECOND WEEK OF LENT
Dn 9:4-10 and Lk 6:36-38

Picture yourself watching a carousel in motion. You look to
the right and see the horses going past, their tails disappearing
around the circle. Then look to the left and see their heads coming
into view again. That's an illustration of the saying we often hear,
namely, "What goes round, comes round." The same image is
being taught in today's Gospel passage. Jesus says that what we
send into the lives of others will eventually come back into our
own lives. When we cast our bread on the water, it eventually
comes back to us. If we send out to others kindness, friendliness
and forgiveness, then we have God's promise that it will come
back to us in kind. If we send hatred, pain and evil, we should
expect to receive the same in return. It's all so clear and stated so
simply. "Judge and you will be judged. Condemn and you will be
condemned. Pardon and you will be pardoned." This doesn't
mean that God will necessarily repay us with our own conduct but
other people very well may. We might fool some for a little while,
but eventually we will be known for what we are and repaid
accordingly.

TUESDAY OF THE SECOND WEEK OF LENT
Is 1:10, 16-20 and Mt 23:1-12

Jesus makes a truly noble statement in this Gospel when he
tells his apostles to respect the offices held by the scribes and

Pharisees. Although they were his avowed enemies, Jesus separates the people from their positions. Even if he doesn't approve of the people, he can still support their positions and ask his disciples to do likewise. They are to be treated with respect because their office, which was passed down from Moses, deserves it. How many of us can make that fine distinction between the office and the person who occupies it? We would do well to examine our own degree of reverence for the various offices in today's society. It's very easy to pronounce wholesale condemnation on both the position and the person without distinguishing between the two. Maybe we are not enamored with the pope or some bishops or priests, but the offices are to be honored. The office of President and the seats of Congress are worthy of deep respect. The positions of parents, teachers, police personnel, etc., are most deserving of our support and esteem, regardless of who occupies them. Every legitimate office and position carries with it a certain degree of value and dignity.

WEDNESDAY OF THE SECOND WEEK OF LENT
Jr 18:18-20 and Mt 20:17-28

Mothers are naturally vitally concerned about the well-being of their children. It is often stated, sometimes humorously, that Jewish mothers have a unique concern for the success and good fortune of their offspring. In this Gospel, Matthew tells of a Jewish mother who is very anxious about the future of her two boys. These two, James and John, just happened to be disciples of Jesus. Being a simple disciple in God's Kingdom wasn't exactly what she had in mind for them. She wanted them to have the highest positions possible. Her intense concern was taken directly to Jesus, interrupting a very serious conversation. Our Lord was about to discuss his coming passion and death, but the intrusion by Mrs. Zebedee side-tracked him from the subject and he never did return to it. Notice that she does not ask that her two sons be given exalted positions at the right and left hand of Jesus. She demands it: "Promise me," she says. Obviously she did not get her wish. The young men did get fine positions, were successful in their service of the Lord, and ultimately became great saints. We continue to sing their praises today. And their mother, too, has found a place in history. More importantly, Jesus went on to Jerusalem where he died, rose and brought us salvation so that we can sit with God in that heavenly Kingdom.

THURSDAY OF THE SECOND WEEK OF LENT
Jr 17:5-10 and Lk 16:19-31

Jeremiah answers an important question in this passage: "How does trusting in God affect my life?" The famous prophet explains that if a person doesn't have deep trust, then such a one is living like a barren bush in the desert. There is no change of season for such an individual. All is as in a lava waste and there is no source of strength to be found outside of oneself. If a person does have strong faith, it's like living near fresh running water. There the person can stay young and healthy. Contrast the dry, barren bush in the lava waste with the healthy young apple tree displaying its white blossoms and promising delicious red apples. Sin, rejection and selfishness provide us with no nourishment for our life. It's similar to living in a lava waste. Grace, love and friendship provide us nourishment for the day and fruitfulness for many years to come. Jeremiah speaks of us when he says, "More tortuous than all else is the human heart." Our hearts are pulled in many directions. May they always, like the roots of the healthy tree, be drawn to the life giving waters of grace which are to be found in Jesus.

FRIDAY OF THE SECOND WEEK OF LENT
Gn 37:3-4, 12-13, 17-28 and Mt 21:33-43, 45-46

In the *Merchant of Venice,* Shakespeare refers to "shudder-ing fear and green-ey'd jealousy." Those terms rather accurately describe the scene in this passage from Genesis. Joseph, inno-cently and most unexpectedly, encounters the "green ey'd jealousy" of his very own brothers. Their jealousy is so vicious they literally want to kill him. Their anger-filled threats and physical violence had to generate within Joseph a "shuddering fear" for his very life. Our worst enemies in the world today are not fires, floods, wild beasts, diseases, hunger or the devil. Our worst enemies are each other. More pain and hurt come to people from those close to them than from any other source. The world continues to kill its dreamers out of anger and jealousy. Joseph's life was spared but he was sold for twenty pieces of silver. Many centuries later, Jesus would be sold for thirty pieces of silver. Both were stripped of their cloaks. Have I ever attempted to strip my brothers and sisters of their dignity because of my "green ey'd jealousy"?

SATURDAY OF THE SECOND WEEK OF LENT
Mi 7:14-15, 18-20 and Lk 15:1-3, 11-32

Today we heard one of the most famous parables in the entire Bible. It's the story of the man with two sons. It is one of Jesus' most original tales. We normally refer to it as the Parable of the Prodigal Son, or, sometimes, as the Story of the Forgiving Father. Actually, it could better and more properly be called the Parable of the Prodigal Father. His prodigality is much more evident than is that of his son. The father was extremely prodigal with his money when he so easily handed it over to his wayward son. Generally the inheritance would have been conferred on him only after his father's death. The father's "prodigality" is also shown in his total forgiveness of his son when at last he decided to return. It's one of Sacred Scripture's most wonderful commentaries on the relationship of God to his people. As we read again this parable of divine mercy and forgiveness, we are reminded of the lyrics of a modern religious song: "I have loved you with an everlasting love. I have loved you and you are mine." We may have spent much time, effort and money getting ourselves into trouble as did the son in today's Gospel parable. Regardless, we can be assured that God will gladly spend much more to get us out of it. He is truly a Prodigal Father to us all.

MONDAY OF THE THIRD WEEK OF LENT
2 K 5:1-15 and Lk 4:24-30

Both of today's readings speak to the subject of God's broadmindedness in the person of Naaman. He was the Syrian army commander who became the recipient of God's merciful healing. Jesus was totally aware of this man's having been cured of leprosy and, in turn, made comment on the meaning of this healing. Those legally loyal Jewish people became very angry with Jesus as they listened to the virtues of this foreigner being extolled over their own. We, too, can fall into this same sin of narrow-mindedness. Do we think, for example, that Catholics have a monopoly on the whole truth and nothing but the truth, while Protestants, Orthodox, Jewish and other people are all in unyielding error? If we truly feel that way, may God help us. Catholics don't own God; neither do the Protestants or the Jews or any other group. Not even the Fundamentalists can claim exclusive rights to God. God is for all people. The Jews thought that the Messiah would be for the Jews only. Since Jesus did not subscribe to that narrow, nationalistic, racial point of view, the Jews simply refused to accept his claim to Messiahship. We should be glad that God accepts all people equally, for then we can be sure that we're included too.

TUESDAY OF THE THIRD WEEK OF LENT
Dn 3:25, 34-43 and Mt 18:21-35

Today's Gospel is like the story of two brothers, Tom and Bill. Tom had been in prison for twelve years and was finally released. He wanted to come back to his old home town and visit his brother Bill. They agreed to meet in the bar of the local Holiday Inn. Tom came a bit early and waited for two hours for that "quick drink," they were going to share. Bill didn't show. Discouraged, Tom looked at his watch, got up and walked out into the night. Bill had been there the whole time, sitting in the dark near the video games. He was remembering all the previous pain and embarrassment that Tom had caused him and his family. Soon he, too, got up and went home to his family. He never saw his brother Tom again. We often think of forgiveness as limited to three times. Jesus said it should be seventy times seven times. Maybe we can't forget but still we can forgive. It's expected of us. I will meet many of my brothers and sisters today. To some of them, I don't speak anymore because of past hurts. Couldn't I find at least one more "hello" to offer them as I pass by?

WEDNESDAY OF THE THIRD WEEK OF LENT
Dt 4:1, 5-9 and Mt 5:17-19

Moses is absolutely amazed that God is so close to the people of Israel. He makes sure that they all appreciate this fact and wants them to know that God is not that close to any other nation. The young especially, he says, must understand this closeness of God and never forget it. The Greek's view of God was someone to be feared. They felt that God had to be constantly appeased. And even that would not necessarily make God love a person. God would do whatever he wanted and answered to no one. God did not have to be logical. Moses says that the God of Israel is not only close to them, but very just and kind to them as well. The amazing thing is that these theological ideas were being expressed 1300 years before the birth of Jesus. What, I wonder, would Moses say of our relationship to Jesus? Talk about God's being close to his people! Jesus took on our weak human nature and spiritually dwells within us. We should be much more excited about this relationship than Moses was. We have a happy tale to tell about a divine and human love affair. Make sure your children and grandchildren hear and appreciate this lovely story of God and his people.

THURSDAY OF THE THIRD WEEK OF LENT
Jr 7:23-28 and Lk 11:14-23

Today marks the half-way point in the season of Lent. Twenty days have passed and there are twenty more to go. It's a proper day to pause to make a brief survey of our current spiritual journey. We can look back to our accomplishments and ahead to our yet unfulfilled goals. At this vantage point, we have 20-20 vision. Perhaps a mid-course correction is called for in our Lenten mission. In conjunction with today's Gospel, it might be fitting to examine our inner selves to determine if we have removed any of the devils from our lives. Have we continued to uphold our resolutions and relied on the hand of God to direct us? The example Jesus gives of the strong, fully armed guard protecting the courtyard makes an excellent analogy to our spiritual struggles. Jesus is the armed guard of our souls who protects us from the advances of evil powers which, without God's grace, we are unable to conquer. In this regard, we have perpetual protection, since the Lord Jesus promised to be with us always. We need not fear the evil spirits because of the promise of Jesus being on guard in our behalf. Stand firm.

FRIDAY OF THE THIRD WEEK OF LENT
Ho 14:2-10 and Mk 12:28-34

Among the ancient Jews, there were often heated discussions as to which commandment was really the most important. They called it the "parent commandment." The school of Hillel would say one thing and the school of Gamaliel, another. In that atmosphere, it would be expected that someone would ask Jesus his opinion. The question today came from a scribe — a secretary who was knowledgeable in such matters. Jesus prefaces his remarks with the usual prophetic introductory phrase, "Hear, O Israel." It's like the term used in court, "Hear ye, hear ye," when an important announcement is about to be made. Jesus sounds the "Hear, O Israel," and then makes his important announcement. It is that we are to love God with all our hearts and our neighbor just as much. Therefore, it is not possible for us to have a genuine true love of God and still neglect our neighbor. It is the nature of God-like love that it cannot be given only to one and not to another. Nor can a person run out of love by giving too much of it away. In giving all our love to God, we have that much more for our neighbor. Nor can we give it all to our neighbor without, simultaneously, giving it all to God. Jesus says, "What you do for others, you do for me."

SATURDAY OF THE THIRD WEEK OF LENT
Ho 6:1-6 and Lk 18:9-14

Luke alone tells the parable contrasting the self-righteous Pharisee with the humble tax collector. The characters are, of course, stereotyped as is the case in most parables, to make a point clearly and dramatically. The underlying and unstated question being addressed here is: How is a person saved? Do we attain salvation by strictly observing the external laws of religion, or by believing in God's eternal love and mercy? The Pharisee was law-centered. He fasted two days a week, Monday and Thursday, even from water. He also tithed his income to the Lord. If one fasts two days each week, that's 29% of your time fasting. The Pharisee does not see himself as God's servant in humility, but since he does his "duties," God "must" be pleased and love him very much. In a sense, God becomes his servant, for he pays his generous dues to him for this purpose — 10% of his money and 29% of his time. The tax collector, on the other hand, knows he is unable to save himself by anything that he might do. And he understands that he cannot command God's love. What can he do, then? Beg for mercy. He prays with the helplessness and dependency of a little child. God truly loves this trusting tax collector for this and sends him home — a justified man.

MONDAY OF THE FOURTH WEEK OF LENT
Is 65:17-21 and Jn 4:43-54

The Gospel today presents us with another dramatic story of the power of faith. It was told by our Lord early in his ministry in his native surroundings of northern Galilee. Actually, it is the second miracle of Cana. Between the first and the second miracle which took place in that area, Jesus had ministered briefly in Jerusalem and Samaria. Now, he has returned home with the growing reputation of a wonder worker. The royal official from Capernaum had heard of the healing powers of Jesus and was convinced that his abilities were authentic. So, precisely in order to see Jesus, he makes a ten mile trip to Cana and there requests a cure for his very sick son. Jesus had just returned from Jerusalem and now the official asks him to come north to Capernaum. Jesus does not go but rather introduces a new concept into the idea of miracle working. He says that it is not necessary for him to be physically present to effect the cure, and promises to perform a long-distance miracle. The official's faith is strong enough to accept the verbal promise made to him and returns home to find his son completely cured. It had occurred at 1:00 p.m., the very hour when Jesus had spoken to him. Today we might take the occasion of this Gospel to offer a sincere prayer that someone we know might be healed. We might even offer our prayer at 1:00 p.m. in memory of this second Cana miracle.

TUESDAY OF THE FOURTH WEEK OF LENT
Ezk 47:1-9, 12 and Jn 5:1-3, 5-16

The biblical story of creation does not mention the origin of wind and water. They are found present and working together when the Genesis account begins. The wind (spirit) gives life, shape and movement to the otherwise formless water. In the Exodus from Egypt, the wind and water are again working in unison. The wind opened a road through the sea and when the Israelites had crossed, the wind travelled on ahead of them. It was then that the water rushed back to its formless state, thereby destroying the Egyptians. In today's first reading, Ezekiel is seen wading out into the rising stream, being cleansed and reborn in the spirit-filled water flowing from the temple. A man in the Gospel, sick for thirty-eight years, waits by the pool for an angel to stir the water with the wind of the spirit. He wants to experience the flow on his crippled body as it brings him a long-awaited cure. God's healing powers are present in many elements of creation and used especially by our sacramental signs and symbols. Spirit and water, for example, continue to cleanse in the sacrament of baptism. Today's readings can help us appreciate the spiritual significance of these signs by which God touches and heals us through the flow of spirit-filled water.

WEDNESDAY OF THE FOURTH WEEK OF LENT
Is 49:8-15 and Jn 5:17-30

Whenever we are depressed or physically hurting, we can turn to the Prophet Isaiah and find some uplifting thoughts. The section read today is one of his best. It overflows with confidence, courage and a bright vision for the future. It is God's covenant with the people which makes the prophet so upbeat. Restoration is seen for the land; freedom is promised for prisoners and food for the hungry has already been ordered. God's love is promised to the people and not only for a short time, but for eternity. Love is eternal. This passage concludes with the famous verse which Fr. Carroll Stuhlmueller, C.P. says is "perhaps the most touching expression of divine love in the entire Bible." The popular line is prefaced by God who is speaking of the delicate, yet powerful, bond between a mother and her child. Even if a mother's love might be defective, God promises that his love will always endure. Those five memorable words are, "I will never forget you." This quality of divine love is so superior to our human equivalent that it should properly be known by another name. Our love for others often rises and falls with our moods and circumstances. God promises a love which is complete, consistent and everlasting.

THURSDAY OF THE FOURTH WEEK OF LENT
Ex 32:7-14 and Jn 5:31-47

Jesus is seen in this Gospel passage pleading for affirmation from his contemporaries. He wants them to accept him with the same allegiance they gave to Moses centuries earlier. Moses had acknowledged the coming of the Messiah and Jesus reminds them of that. "It was about me that he wrote," Jesus says. Imagine how the people would have adored and praised Jesus had they been present at the transfiguration where Moses appeared along with Elijah. Jesus also reminds the people of how avidly they accepted John the Baptizer as a saintly prophet. John had personally pointed to Jesus as the "lamb of God," and John had told his own disciples to follow Jesus as their new leader. Today we hold Jesus in the highest possible esteem. But when these Gospel events were unfolding, Jesus had not yet fully revealed his true identity. What would have been our reaction to Jesus had we been his contemporaries? It's easy to profess our faith at this time, after his identity has been soundly established. All the more do we admire the deep faith of John the Baptizer who firmly believed in Jesus before the Lord personally gave him any solid reasons for doing so. How strongly do you now believe in the words of Jesus which have not yet been fulfilled?

FRIDAY OF THE FOURTH WEEK OF LENT
Ws 2:1. 12-22 and Jn 7:1-2. 10. 25-30

John the Apostle, who was with Jesus during the last days of his ministry, recounts how Jesus was a marked man whom people were trying to kill. Imagine the Lord God himself forced into a position of having to hide. He even had to disguise the meaning of his words in order to protect himself. When asked if he were going to the Feast of Booths in Jerusalem, he said, "No," meaning "Not publicly." It seems that, on this trip, he was intending to sit in the back row rather than to be up front in the pulpit. This event reveals something of the heart of Jesus. Fearing for his life and intending to remain as anonymous as possible, he was unable to stay quiet or hidden for long. There must have been a powerful force within Jesus which compelled him to speak out and state the truth, albeit always with love. Thus, on this occasion, he began preaching, once again drawing a vast and inquiring crowd which provoked more ire and violence from his adversaries. The language becomes confrontational in tone on the part of Jesus and physical violence is threatened against him. A peacemaker at any cost, he was not. As a consistent defender of truth and justice, there has never been a better. We must constantly examine the real strengths of our own convictions, with the Lord's example ever in mind.

SATURDAY OF THE FOURTH WEEK OF LENT
Jr 11:18-20 and Jn 7:40-53

Jesus came to this world to bring us life, grace and wisdom. It was his mission to lead us to the kingdom of heaven. One of the indirect proofs that Jesus truly is God is that he understands our stupidity and tolerates it in his efforts to teach us at least a rudimentary spiritual way of life. One would imagine that Jesus must have sometimes thought of this world in the vein expressed by George Bernard Shaw. He once said, "From the actions of humankind it seems to me as if this particular planet of ours must be the insane asylum for some other world." In this passage Jesus simply wants to teach the people, but they almost immediately become engaged in a major dispute about his credentials. He had told them many times he was a prophet, but they refused to believe. His adversaries manufactured various religious reasons why he wasn't. Humankind is an undisciplined class even for the world's most outstanding teacher. The passage ends with all the participants angrily going to their own separate houses. How much better it would have been had they all gone to the Lord's house and talked to God and each other, thus resolving their differences through mutual understanding.

MONDAY OF THE FIFTH WEEK OF LENT
Dn 13:1-9, 15-17, 19-30, 33-62 and Jn 8:1-11

Jesus deeply respected Moses but reformed many of the old Mosaic laws. One major reform had to do with the law of stoning to death women who were accused of adultery. Jesus defended women and wanted no one's life snuffed out in such a way or for such a reason. The Lord was concerned about people reforming their own lives and finding fulfillment in so doing rather than being put to death for an infraction of the law. His was not an easy message to preach in this often brutal Middle Eastern culture which believed in killing sinners and thus removing them from society. These moral stands taken by our Lord continued to irritate the scribes and Pharisees who had judged Jesus as soft when it came to matters of traditional morality. The Pharisees thought everyone might be encouraged to commit adultery if they followed the Lord's more merciful teachings. Jesus himself died a victim of the harsh morality which he opposed, but his executioners were consistent in what they did for that was the way they solved problems. The teachings of Jesus still are not followed today. So often we continue to think that it is better to kill and remove rather than to forgive and reform.

TUESDAY OF THE FIFTH WEEK OF LENT
Nb 21:4-9 and Jn 8:21-30

Moses, the freedom fighter, led the people away from what they hated most — their detention under slavery. He promised them freedom and was in the midst of accomplishing that objective when his followers began to complain and rebel. The people, running low on patience and tired from the journey each day, said that they were "disgusted with this wretched food." They quickly forgot their days of confined servitude in Egypt and how disgruntled they were under slavery. God's punishment in the form of poisonous serpents quickly brought them to their senses. In the meantime, Moses, the expert leader that he was, simply continued to follow God's long range plan which would eventually bring them to the Promised Land. We are blessed when we have a good leader. The good leader must listen to what is legitimate but ignore the mere whining of the people. The good leader, whether in church, government, business, school or family, must courageously pursue the course which he or she knows is best. Freedom is always high priced and difficult; only the very strong achieve it. Jesus was the strongest and he won the highest freedom.

WEDNESDAY OF THE FIFTH WEEK OF LENT
Dn 3:14-20, 91-92, 95 and Jn 8:31-42

The biblical account of the three men in the fiery furnace is a well-known and often read story from the Old Testament. It was written to give courage to a people who were suffering in dire and seemingly hopeless situations. The three central characters, Shadrach, Meshach and Abednego are commanded to worship a pagan statue and they refuse. They are severely threatened but still refuse. The penalty, torture and death in a white-hot furnace, is then applied. Even though they face the furnace rather than disappoint their God, they do not demand or even pray for God to spare their lives. The cool resignation they display is spiritual "true grit." Their reply is, "If God will save us, that's fine. If not, we will die rather than worship an idol." We clearly get the point that theirs is no good-time faith only and that they don't need a sign from God before they make a life and death commitment. God "danced" with them over the white-hot coals and none of them were injured, for their faith had fire-proofed them. They could face any danger, for now they were not three but four. With grace from above, you can face any odds, for you and God always make a majority.

THURSDAY OF THE FIFTH WEEK OF LENT
Gn 17:3-9 and Jn 8:51-59

The name of a person is often considered to be much more
than simply an artificial label by which we identify a particular
individual. Names have deep meanings, long standing traditions,
personal dignity, a sacred symbolism and certain predictive qualities for those who bear them. Unique attention is given to the
importance of names in both of today's readings. Abram does not
have the right name for the role he will be called upon to play so
his name is altered to better fit his new calling. "Abraham," his
new name, contains the concept of "father." He will become the
father of a new nation and his name will be an everlasting reminder of his destined role. In the Gospel, Jesus is trying to convince
his Jewish hearers that he existed long before Abraham. He says
his name is really, "I Am," i.e., everlasting existence. That name
more clearly signifies his true eternal nature. "Jesus," is his
earthly name. Think of the quality and meaning of your name.
Where did it originate and what does it signify? Remember that at
baptism it was pronounced in the same breath as the Name of the
Father and of the Son and of the Holy Spirit. Our names have been
made holy and thereby give direction to our style of living.

FRIDAY OF THE FIFTH WEEK OF LENT
Jr 20:10-13 and Jn 10:31-42

Jesus says that if the people refuse to believe in his words,
they should at least accept his deeds. The Lord is applying here
the old saying that works speak louder than words. A person
might say, "I believe that God exists." That is a clear and forceful
statement. A stronger declaration would be, "I, indeed, believe
that God exists." If I, "in deed," believe, it means that I express
my belief in the way I act and, therefore, I am expressing a much

strong faith. What we do — our deeds — are much more telling of us than what we say — our words. There is a story of an old lady dying who, for fifty years, had done volunteer work for needy people. Her pastor of many years was now present at her bedside. To him, she expressed some fear. "What will I tell the Master when I see him?" Her pastor calmly replied, "Don't say anything. Just show him your hands." Perhaps God is more impressed by the work of our hands than the sound of our voice. God's voice is heard most clearly not in sounds from heaven but in the fullness of created splendor. Note how Eucharistic Prayers Two and Three begin with, "Lord Father you are holy *indeed*," Today, let us ask for the grace to forget the words and be holy in deed.

SATURDAY OF THE FIFTH WEEK OF LENT
Ezk 37:21-28 and Jn 11:45-57

Julius Irving (Dr. J.) will long be remembered as an outstanding star in professional basketball. Once, following an exciting victory for the '76ers, in which Dr. J. sank the winning shot, he was asked to express his feelings. He would take no particular credit for the victory. "I don't brag when we win," he said, "and I don't cry when we lose." Jesus, like a seasoned athlete, maintained a constant calmness in his heart in the heat of many encounters. He was well aware that his words, actions and miracles would generate both devoted love and intense hatred and jealousy. He brought Lazarus back to life and that brought a crowd of curious onlookers to Bethany to "investigate" this miracle. Some wanted to follow Jesus; others wanted to kill him. Jesus neither bragged about the victory over death nor cried over the threats of his opponents. He was a symbol of hope and at the same time a sign to be contradicted. His followers must have the same attitude. We cannot equally please all people. Jesus couldn't either. Had Jesus wanted to peacefully accommodate himself to everyone, he could not have been the Messiah. Nor can we be true Christians.

MONDAY OF HOLY WEEK
Is 42:1-7 and Jn 12:1-11

It's only a couple of miles from Jerusalem to Bethany following the caravan road. Jesus must have gone there often to visit. We clearly recall the one day he was there when Martha complained about Mary's sitting at his feet and not helping with the housework. Jesus came back another time to raise their brother Lazarus from the dead. Today's Gospel places Jesus back in Bethany once more, this time to celebrate a "return to life" party for Lazarus. Notice how everyone is doing what he or she does best. Martha is serving the meal. Lazarus is simply sitting there quietly — he never speaks in the Scriptures. Mary is again at the feet of Jesus, anointing them with oil, while Jesus is leisurely addressing the assembled guests. Everyone is acting naturally, doing the things they most enjoy and sharing with one another. We, too, are people of many divergent tastes. Our natural and spiritual talents are different, but they are all gifts to the community. Jesus did not expect Lazarus to anoint his feet with perfumed oil, or Mary to prepare the lunch, or Martha to sit calmly at his feet and talk. It's a wonderful picture of how we should all be in the presence of the Lord — simply ourselves and feeling good about it.

TUESDAY OF HOLY WEEK
Is 49:1-6 and Jn 13:21-33, 36-38

Jesus, normally in command of every situation, is now, according to John, "deeply troubled." Can we picture Jesus in this agitated state of mind and body? Did he break out in a sweat, sigh, or shake his hands in his anxiety? Did his voice quiver when he tried to speak? As we think about Jesus' being deeply troubled, we ask ourselves, "Why?" This time it's not the Pharisees who are bothering him. It seems that there is a serious problem within his own group — Judas. His former close friend is about to betray him. The disciples are going to be shocked when they realize what is about to happen and who's going to do it. The betrayal will lead Jesus to vicious suffering and death. Jesus knew it ahead of time and was deeply troubled by it. He speaks of his death to Peter, saying, "I am going where you cannot follow me now; later on you shall come after me." Peter did, indeed, follow the Lord when he was martyred and Jesus was there to assist him to victory. That "later on" date will eventually be a reality in all our lives. When it approaches we, too, will probably be deeply troubled. It helps to know that Jesus promised to be with us when our time to die approaches. We thank God for this final grace.

WEDNESDAY OF HOLY WEEK
Is 50:4-9 and Mt 26:14-25

Today's Gospel offers us four brief meditations for our consideration. The first of these is on *Greed.* It's not stated, but strongly implied, that Judas would not have betrayed Jesus had he not been paid. A piece of silver was a Jewish shekel, worth about 64 cents. The price placed on the head of Jesus amounted to something less than $20.00. The second has to do with *Mystery.* There's a "mystery man" in the Gospel passage we just heard. Mark and Luke say that this man would be carrying a pitcher of water. He'll be easy to spot for women usually carried the water in those days. The disciples were to follow this man to some house. No address is given. The man with the pitcher remains one of the nameless friends of Jesus. Third, there is the matter of

Tension. Here was a divided table, a stress-filled supper. The disciples were distressed with the way Jesus was talking. The statement, "Better for him had he not been born," only heightened the anxiety. Goodness and evil sat down to dine at the same table. And finally, there was *Deception.* Judas says to Jesus, "Surely, it is not I, Rabbi?" About to strike a deadly blow, he addresses Jesus with a title of respect and feigns his own innocence. It then grew dark.

HOLY THURSDAY
Ex 12:1-8, 11-14; 1 Cor 11:23-36 and Jn 13:1-15

We are beginning to notice again the sights and sounds of spring as we celebrate the anniversary of the First Mass. Christians all over the world are joyfully gathering in their churches this evening to hear again the Scripture stories of salvation and to join in the religious ceremonies. The Apostle John retells how Jesus washed the feet of his disciples. This is a type of parable, not of words but example. The Lord did what a servant would normally do. Then he tells us, "Do the same for each other." The point is direct and clear. The bread is blessed and broken for our salvation. We can never forget the blessed physical body of Jesus which was broken for us. We consecrate the bread and wine in memory of him. The author, Leslie Weatherhead, tells of a frail ten-year-old boy whose mother died and he was admitted to a Children's Home run by some Sisters. The first thing they did was give him a warm shower and clean clothes. He loved the new outfit but put on his old tattered cap. He clutched it tightly when the sisters tried to remove it. After coaxing, he exchanged it for a new one. But, before accepting the new one, he ripped the lining from the old and stuffed it in his pocket. "Why did you do that?" Sister asked. "Because," he replied, "that's part of my mother's dress. I must keep it to remember her." Jesus said, "Do this in memory of me."

GOOD FRIDAY
Is 52:13 - 53:12; Heb 4:14-16; 5:7-9 and Jn 18:1 - 19:42

One of the songs Burl Ives made popular is entitled: "Four
Initials on a Tree." The story is about a man coming back to his
home town and walking past his old high school. He sees a tree
where he and his girl friend, years ago, had carved their initials.
They drifted apart then but the initials are still there. The lyrics go
something like: "Four initials on a tree, still there for all to see.
Four initials on a tree, that's all that's left of love." On Good
Friday and Easter Sunday every year, many people just drift back
into church for a little visit. Perhaps it's a tug of conscience or a bit
of nostalgia that brings them there. Maybe they remember an old
love affair with the Lord when they were young. We can all
remember those years as children when we did so much for Jesus
— our little deeds done out of deep faith and high ideals. Then
came the drifting years. We forgot about our promise to love
Jesus to the end of time — and beyond. Notice that those four
initials are still there today on the tree of the cross: J N R J, *Jesus
Nazarenus Rex Judaeorum,* Jesus of Nazareth, King of the Jews.
For us he died to keep his promise of eternal love. If our love for
him has grown cold, we can rekindle it again, for true love is
everlasting. Listen! You may hear him saying, "I would like to
renew with you today an old friendship!" Signed, J N R J.

THE EASTER SEASON

MONDAY OF THE OCTAVE OF EASTER
Ac 2:14, 22-32 and Mt 28:8-15

This is a very curious Gospel passage and one which is unique to Matthew. Here he engages in a bit of investigative reporting. Matthew says that Jesus rose from the dead. The Jewish guards say he did not rise, but that his body was stolen by the apostles who reported a resurrection. Matthew's solution is that the guards lied because they were bribed to do so by the chief priests and elders. Since the bribe was obviously kept secret we can only speculate how Matthew became aware of it. He is very confident in reporting a secret meeting between the chief priest and the guards to concoct the story and pay them the hush money. Perhaps Matthew, the one-time public official of the government, consulted some of his former fellow workers and friends to obtain this inside information. We see here the tremendous power of money to manipulate people. Money makes the guards say that they were asleep — a criminal offense for which they could have been court-martialed — although Matthew clearly states that they were completely awake as they were expected to be. They witnessed the descent of a brilliant angel and were absolutely terrified. Still, they were more impressed by the power of money than they were with the power of God who raised Jesus from the tomb.

TUESDAY OF THE OCTAVE OF EASTER
Ac 2:36-41 and Jn 20:11-18

Jesus asks Mary Magdalene two questions: "Why are you weeping?" and "Who is it you are looking for?" The questions are asked, not as a traveler requesting a street address or building location, but as a teacher asking questions from a student. The

Lord is always coaxing a faith expression from his believing
people. Mary is challenged here to put her feelings into words
and, thereby, be even more definite and clear about her true
convictions. Mary quickly sees that it is truly Jesus. She understands and refers to him as teacher. Jesus is our Savior and
teacher who uses the same approach to elicit the best from us.
We, too, should be able to shout out as Mary did, "I have seen the
Lord." What does the Risen Lord actually look like? We would
have to know in order to say we have seen the Lord. Mary
Magdalene knew Jesus well but at first she saw only the gardener
— then she saw Jesus. We, too, are to see God in the gardener,
janitor, cab driver, waitress, factory worker and in all ordinary
men and women. When we see them as our brothers and sisters,
then we have seen the Risen Lord.

WEDNESDAY OF THE OCTAVE OF EASTER
Ac 3:1-10 and Lk 24:13-35

Today we are on the road with Jesus and two friends in the
famous seven-mile walk to Emmaus. With his terrible pain and
agonizing death behind him, Jesus is now having a joyful time with
his new resurrected body. His subtle sense of humor surfaces in
the question, "What things are you discussing?" His own death
and resurrection is the topic of their discussion and he is well
aware of it. Yet, as in the case of Mary Magdalene, his question is
meant to draw out their faith and have them express it clearly in
words. He is very direct with his words, reminding them of their
lack of faith and what little sense they have. Imagine the amazement of the two disciples as this "stranger" explains the
Scriptures to them. They are especially impressed with his profound knowledge of the Messiah. The Risen Lord is discovered
again in the breaking of the bread. It has become his trademark.
Then he disappeared. Jesus has disappeared into our bread only

to reappear again in the lives and good works of his people. Whether on the altar or on the road, the Lord is not far from those who believe.

THURSDAY OF THE OCTAVE OF EASTER
Ac 3:11-26 and Lk 24:35-48

Jesus said that ghosts don't have bones and they don't eat fish. He wanted his disciples to appreciate his bones and his appetite, for these would prove to them both his physical reality and his humanness. This is a rather clear statement by Jesus about his human nature and an expression of pride in his physical qualities. We, too, are expected to appreciate our human nature and all the physical qualities we possess. That is also being very religious and spiritual. Being Christlike or spiritual doesn't mean we must act in some aloof or strange way. The more we think and act with common sense, in a balanced human way, the more we are like Christ. It's another way of restating the old principle of the supernatural being built on the natural. We, like Jesus, are not ghosts or spirits. We, like Jesus, get hungry and must eat. Some things we feel in our minds and hearts and other things we feel in our bones. That's the way we are made. The Lord became truly human for our benefit and that remains our strongest and most consistent link to the Almighty. We should never apologize for being only a human. We are human and physically real and in that we rejoice.

FRIDAY OF THE OCTAVE OF EASTER
Ac 4:1-12 and Jn 21:1-14

The disciples were going fishing, but not for relaxation. That had been their former job and, at this point, they were confused about Jesus. They had been separated from the Lord for the first time in three years and who knew if and when he would return? They needed to work in order to eat. Their faith at this time was really being put to the test. Jesus takes them to task for their unbelief and addresses them as children. It must have been a term these grown men of the sea did not appreciate. Yet, in the ways of faith and spirituality they were but children. Jesus further demonstrates how little they knew even about fishing. The Lord, considered the amateur fisherman, directs the "professionals" to the spot where the fish are. They are told to lower the net on the right. There's always a right way to do anything. The power of this passage is that Jesus is a total leader in all the areas of life. This is the second time they are called out of the water and out of the fishing boats to become full-time disciples. Mass and breakfast follow on the beach. The Lord calls us as full-time followers and shows us the right way to pray, work and live.

SATURDAY OF THE OCTAVE OF EASTER
Ac 4:13-21 and Mk 16:9-15

The poet, Alexander Pope, says in one of his famous rhyming couplets: "Be not the first by whom the new is tried, Nor yet the last to lay the old aside." That advice could give some direction to the situation in this reading from the Acts of the Apostles. The passage is filled with tension as the old religious ways and the news ones vie for dominance. The Jewish priests and elders want to believe and pass on to future generations their sacred teachings and traditions. The Apostles, Peter and John, are just as determined to tell the world about the teachings of Jesus. The outward signs, the enthusiasm and popular acceptance are all on the side of the Apostles. Judaism has its long-standing traditions in its favor but the leaders fear that these could be eroded by the current Christian excitement. Religious changes, by their very nature, come slowly and only with much contention. Often, as is seen here, the objective truths which should be followed are sacrificed in favor of personal benefits. Favorable happenings can not be denied by some, nor accepted by others. We, like the Apostles, must speak and witness to the truths as we see and experience them. Both yesterday and tomorrow must make some concessions that today can be liveable.

MONDAY OF THE SECOND WEEK OF EASTER
Ac 4:23-31 and Jn 3:1-8

Today we meet Nicodemus, the friendly Pharisee. The Pharisees, no doubt, were friendly to many people but they did not extend their loving congeniality to Jesus. Their defensive hostility is found smoldering on numerous pages of the New Testament. Nicodemus was the exception. Although law-centered, like his contemporaries, he could appreciate the spirit-centered teachings of Jesus. Nicodemus did much more than tolerate Jesus. He supported him as an outstanding teacher from God. In that capacity he came to Jesus at night to inquire about his doctrine of baptism. He spoke publicly in court in behalf of Jesus, reminding the Lord's accusers that he deserved a fair trial. Finally, it was Nicodemus who managed to follow Jesus to Calvary and be present at his burial, bringing a large quantity of costly spices. Speculation is that he was later baptized and became a Christian. Nicodemus was reminded by Jesus that the spiritual world, like the blowing wind, is invisible, but it has a distinct superiority over the finite world of material objects. It is in the spiritual world we find God's kingdom. Jesus counsels us as he did the friendly Pharisee, to be "begotten of the Spirit."

TUESDAY OF THE SECOND WEEK OF EASTER
Ac 4:32-37 and Jn 3:7-15

This passage from the Book of Acts tells of a practice in the very early days of the Church in Jerusalem of holding all property in common. We often think of this procedure as an idyllic model of selflessness. Scripture scholars tell us that the common property arrangement didn't last long or work well because of human greed and selfishness. Difficult or not, it did become the litmus test of some early believers in Jesus. Barnabas was one notable who sold his farm to obtain the kingdom. He then became Paul's traveling companion and an outstanding missionary in his own right. Sharing one's material possessions with the community or simply letting go of them for a higher spiritual motive is not an easy feat. It's a difficult decision because there is a tremendous, if basically false, sense of security in having material wealth. Today, we try to encourage a spirituality about giving to the Church. We are called to donate not in a sense of crisis-giving, i.e., if the boiler breaks down and we must pay to have it repaired. We should give in a spirit of stewardship. That means to support the Church with a certain percentage of our means regardless of whether the boiler needs fixing or not.

WEDNESDAY OF THE SECOND WEEK OF EASTER
Ac 5:17-26 and Jn 3:16-21

The Acts of the Apostles is an exciting book about life in the early Church. In today's passage, Luke recounts two significant facts. First, we note that the followers of Jesus were very persistent in their desire to preach. Once, when locked in the public jail, they were miraculously released. Then, simply and immediately, they went back to preaching. They had been freed originally by Jesus through his death and resurrection and they were convinced that the Lord was continuing to provide them with the freedom they needed to speak out. Their zeal was both genuine and inspirational. The second fact worthy of note is that the followers of Jesus originally were not called Christians but were known as those who followed the "Way," and preached a "New Life." In an effort to keep our religious terminology from becoming mere jargon, we might call ourselves the "New Life People." Do we really have a new life in Christ? How is it superior to the old life? We are "New Life People" insofar as we have as our head a New Adam. We read the New Testament. Jesus says we have become a New Creation. And we look forward to a New Day when all will be renewed in Christ. Anyone who professes to follow Jesus cannot be afraid of that which is new.

THURSDAY OF THE SECOND WEEK OF EASTER
Ac 5:27-33 and Jn 3:31-36

Many people today still remember how various items were rationed during the Second World War. These included essential products such as meat, sugar, clothes, gasoline, etc. People were supplied with a certain number of stamps which were necessary for the purchase of these commodities. Some individuals often wanted more of the rationed items but were restricted to the amount which the stamps would permit. In today's reading, Jesus tells Nicodemus that God "does not ration his gift of the Spirit." Spiritual gifts are handed to us in superabundance. We are given more than enough in most every area of our lives. God's trademark is unparalleled generosity. Scripture also assures us that we are given all the graces necessary for success. The implication of this is that we may be poor materially, but there is no excuse for being spiritually destitute. God is seen as a spiritual billionaire with precious gifts of faith, hope, love, patience, perseverance, which he opulently distributes to all. They are not rationed, they are abundant and they are free. Why aren't we more spiritually rich than we are?

FRIDAY OF THE SECOND WEEK OF EASTER
Ac 5:34-42 and Jn 6:1-15

Jesus not only served the vast crowd free bread, but he gave them fish as well. Nor was their meal served buffet-style. It was a sit-down meal. John makes sure we understand that what Jesus does is accomplished with distinctive class. Philip had said that not even two hundred days wages could supply the crowd with enough bread to give everyone a bite. In other words, a huge amount of money would not have satisfied the crowd. They were satisfied only with what Jesus could give them and as always his gift was freely given. This Gospel continues the same theme as yesterday's — God's generosity to his people. Notice that all have eaten and there are still twelve baskets of bread left over. There was one basket of bread for each apostle. They would carry it with them as a symbol of the Church's ministry to the hungry of the world. The bread continues to be multiplied by God's blessings for those who are both physically and spiritually hungry.

SATURDAY OF THE SECOND WEEK OF EASTER
Ac 6:1-7 and Jn 6:16-21

Today we read from the Gospel of John that very familiar passage about Jesus walking on the water. This Scripture story is told by three of the evangelists (Matthew, Mark and John) and all three offer some additional information which the others don't mention. Matthew alone, for example, tells the entire incident of Peter exiting the boat and walking a few steps toward Jesus. Mark adds the brief note that Jesus might have passed them by had they not cried out in fear. John supplies a unique and very interesting detail when he says the apostles had rowed three or four miles when Jesus approached them. Matthew and Mark give the approximate time, at the fourth watch, between 3:00 and 6:00 a.m. When we put together all the pieces, we have a terrific story. One striking conclusion from John's account could be that Jesus walked three or four miles on the water. Matthew implies that Peter's walk on the water consisted of three or four steps. An encouraging spiritual truth is being taught here. In coming to bring us salvation, God is willing to walk a mile for every step we take. Jesus again demonstrates why he truly is our rightful Savior.

MONDAY OF THE THIRD WEEK OF EASTER
Ac 6:8-15 and Jn 6:22-29

We often think of our spiritual duties as divided into two parts — faith and works. When we come to Mass, say a rosary, engage in meditation, etc., we are practicing our faith. If we are feeding the hungry, giving an elderly person a ride to the store or volunteering time for the Red Cross, we are doing good works. Perhaps faith and works should be more united in our thinking. Jesus makes that point in today's Gospel reading. The crowd wants to know "what they must do to perform the works of God." Jesus says that the real work of God is "to have faith in the One whom he has sent." When we have faith and express that faith, we are thereby doing a good work. Right now, as you read or listen to this homily, you are not only deepening your faith but actually doing a good work. It's a repeat of the Martha-Mary syndrome. Martha thought that good works meant being physically busy. Jesus affirmed Mary's view that good works include quiet prayers, meaningful conversations, etc., even though we are physically inactive. Instead of deciding what's faith and what's works, we simply try to faithfully work in all circumstances, regardless of what we are doing.

TUESDAY OF THE THIRD WEEK OF EASTER
Ac 7:51 - 8:1 and Jn 6:30-35

People love to imitate their heroes and heroines. Kids, especially, wear jerseys, shoes, socks, numbers, hairdos, etc., of those they admire in sports, movies and TV. Here in the Acts of the Apostles, we see Stephen caught up in the total imitation of Jesus. He spoke like Jesus against his opposition, calling them "stiff-necked, uncircumcised in heart and ears and opposing the Holy Spirit." In his ecstasy, he saw Jesus standing at God's right hand. Like Jesus, he was dragged outside the city gates and put to death. True also to the style of Jesus, Stephen loudly and explicitly forgave the very people who were killing him. Stephen is the first adult person to accept martyrdom in testimony to the life and teachings of Jesus. He was able to endure, even welcome, the pains of a brutal death because he had only Jesus on his mind. He copied his Master's format in every way possible. We will all have our own manner of living and dying. But to some degree, and in some ways, we are to imitate the life and death of Jesus.

WEDNESDAY OF THE THIRD WEEK OF EASTER
Ac 8:1-8 and Jn 6:35-40

The Acts of the Apostles is a very exciting book and today's passage presents us with a typical slice of the action. Stephen has been killed for his profession of faith in Jesus. The Church is reacting to his martyrdom with a curious mixture of joy for his spiritual victory and a deep sense of personal loss. The atmosphere is alive with anticipation. Paul, who will be a future saint, is currently the Church's most aggressive persecutor. Philip has been energized by the Spirit of God to continue the preaching and other activities which were being done by Stephen. Unclean spirits are being expelled from those possessed, cripples are walking again and other miracles are occurring. Luke describes the entire situation by saying, "The rejoicing in that town rose to fever pitch." When the lector concluded today's reading, our liturgical response of, "Thanks be to God," should have been a resounding one and not a weak mumble. The Church hopes that we will carry this same energized spirit of Stephen out to the streets, to our jobs and homes and to the marketplace in general. God's life abides within our souls causing us to laugh, cry, argue, suffer and express our views as did the first generation of Christians.

THURSDAY OF THE THIRD WEEK OF EASTER
Ac 8:26-40 and Jn 6:44-51

Bread and water are two of the most basic forms of food and drink which we possess. If we had to reduce our physical intake to the most elementary level, we would be left with these two. This same concept is carried over into our religious thinking and both are highlighted in today's liturgical readings. The Ethiopian servant of the queen is instructed in the faith and wants the fresh, life-giving water of baptism poured over him. "Look, there is some water right there. What is to keep me from being baptized?" That is the same fashion in which we were all spiritually reborn. The water of baptism must flow over our heads as the first sacrament we receive. Jesus, in this Gospel, proclaims himself to be "the bread that came down from heaven." He is the living bread which provides the nourishment needed for a deep spiritual life to those who reverently receive him. Water and bread — baptism and Eucharist — in that order, sustain both our physical and our spiritual lives.

FRIDAY OF THE THIRD WEEK OF EASTER
Ac 9:1-20 and Jn 6:52-59

One of the elementary guidelines for daily living is the Golden Rule. There are different variations of the idea of doing to others as we would have them do to us. Jesus reminds us in the Acts of the Apostles that what we do to others we do to him. Today's reading emphasizes the negative point of view — what we do against others is also done against the Lord. In this passage, Paul is shown as a persecutor of the early Christians when he hears the voice of Jesus ask, "Why are you persecuting *me?*" It can be sobering to acknowledge that all our gossip, degrading talk and poking fun of others is also directed against the Lord. Paul, who at this point is still called Saul, has his name called twice. There is no doubt that he was the one being addressed and told to stop persecuting Jesus. The experience leaves Paul blind and shaken. We, too, can be blinded to what we are doing and to how much harm we are causing, even by our diminutive jabs and little digs. When we have offended another, we need not only apologize to that person but also to the Lord, for the offense was a dual violation.

SATURDAY OF THE THIRD WEEK OF EASTER
Ac 9:31-42 and Jn 6:60-69

"Lord, to whom shall we go?" St. Peter's famous question followed a previous question from Jesus. He had asked the Twelve if they wanted to leave his company? Many disciples had already walked away, and Jesus didn't want people staying if they thought they should leave. Peter and the others told Jesus they didn't want to abandon him for they were convinced that he came from God and had the words of eternal life. If we left Jesus and the teachings of the Gospel, where would we go? To whom would we turn? What would we find as a substitute to fill the void? It's a haunting question. In 1981, World Library publications published a song composed by Eugene Englert entitled "Lord, to Whom Shall We Go?" The lyrics are given a melody which follows the thoughts expressed. For example, the word "go" in the refrain is sung on the lowest note. It would be a low point, indeed, for the Apostles or for us to walk off and leave Jesus. The song, taking its cue from the Psalms, then goes on to express some reasons for staying: "to do God's will is my delight; my soul longs for God . . . and only there do I find rest and salvation."

MONDAY OF THE FOURTH WEEK OF EASTER
Ac 11:1-18 and Jn 10:1-10

"Smoking or non-smoking?" That's a question being asked often these days when one enters a restaurant and certain other places of assembly. Thankfully, the matter of whether one is black or white is no longer a determining factor of where one can sit or stand in a public establishment, even though some vestiges of prejudice do still remain. In biblical times the ethical question was: "Are you circumcised or not?" If not, one would be regarded as unclean and hence to be avoided. Genesis 17:14 decreed that an uncircumcised person was separated from the covenant. Jewish converts to Christianity thought it would be necessary for all males to be circumcised before they could be received into the Church which had its roots in Judaism. The decision at the Council of Jerusalem was that Gentile converts did not have to follow the Mosaic law in this regard. Here, in a vision, Peter is told not to make distinctions between people or to segregate them into classes: circumcised vs. uncircumcised, clean vs. unclean. Jesus died and rose for all indiscriminately. Since all have been redeemed in his blood, no one is to consider himself or herself better than another. We still need to be reminded that "what God has purified we are not to call unclean."

TUESDAY OF THE FOURTH WEEK OF EASTER
Ac 11:19-26 and Jn 10:22-30

History has documented the beginning of the Church and traced its journey through the centuries and across the continents. We now can read and study that unfinished story of progress. In its early years, there was no clear vision of the precise direction the Church should go and who should belong to it. There was a common belief that the Christian Church was meant for Jewish people only. Likewise, it was felt that the Church was to function within Israel with its ruling body in Jerusalem. Soon spiritual inspirations began influencing the leaders, such as the message which came to Peter in a vision negating the stigma of being labeled unclean. Early discussions with the Greeks found them interested in joining. The Church almost immediately expanded beyond the borders of Israel. The vast scope of its mission was rapidly taking shape. Help was needed and that brought Paul on the scene. He imaginatively accelerated its expansion in undreamed of ways. In our day the Second Vatican Council initiated a process, continued in the Synods of Bishops, for charting the direction of the Church in the twenty-first century. We have seen a lot of debate and not a little confusion just as when the Church began. But gradually, things get clarified. The guiding principles remain the same: the Church is for all, without class or distinction. Some are not "more clean" than others.

WEDNESDAY OF THE FOURTH WEEK OF EASTER
Ac 12:24 - 13:5 and Jn 12:44-50

So often we hear complaints about the many changes in the Church. Certainly the centuries have witnessed numerous alterations, but those are to be expected. It is even more fascinating that so many practices have remained the same through the Church's 2000 years. Notice in our reading from the Acts of the Apostles how the early members of the Church conducted their lives and how similar they were to our own. They met regularly in a prayerful atmosphere to celebrate the liturgy. We still meet and pray in that same setting of the liturgy of the Mass. They also fasted to make sure that they were properly disciplined. We do the same before Communion and at certain times of the year, making a special effort to control the body in order to elevate the mind. The early Christians prayed often as we do. We, like them, seek enlightenment from the word of God rather than from the pundits of the world when trying to give direction to our lives. The sense of tradition ought to be palpable to us every time we meet to celebrate the Holy Sacrifice of the Mass, fast before Holy Communion, or ask the Spirit for guidance.

THURSDAY OF THE FOURTH WEEK OF EASTER
Ac 13:13-25 and Jn 13:16-20

When called upon to speak to the people, Paul gives a long historical account of the many events which happened to the Hebrews. Names, places and events easily flow from his learned tongue. It's a clear sign that these were very meaningful to him, not just in a speculative way, but as an essential part of his own personal religious beliefs. Little did Paul realize that his own name would soon be added to this impressive list of all time greats. It was, no doubt, his extraordinary understanding of the past which so enlightened him for the future. It is said that Pope John XXIII, like Paul, had a very keen sense of history. His understanding of the past gave him both enlightenment and courage to launch the Catholic Church into a new direction, with a renewed spirit, when he convened the Second Vatican Council. He reasoned, as did Paul, that God is faithfully consistent. The principles of the past are valid for the future. Personally, we may be able to get a clear picture of what lies ahead by examining closely those things which have already occurred. History not only reveals but also predicts.

FRIDAY OF THE FOURTH WEEK OF EASTER
Ac 13:26-33 and Jn 14:1-6

This is a Gospel passage rich in its spiritual significance. The very first line sets the tempo. In it Jesus says very calmly: "Do not let your hearts be troubled." Those are seven very powerful words. They are not just a vague suggestion about something we can do, but the statement of a biblical command from Jesus. We have a very foolish superstition that we should not speak of the peacefulness of our lives, for so doing might cause us to lose it. That is the origin of the old practice of knocking on wood when we admit our good fortune. The noise of knocking muffles our voice and, therefore, the devilish fairies won't hear what we say and steal away our happiness. We should not feel guilty if we experience some happiness, even though some others may not. Remember, Jesus wants us all to be happy. "I came that my joy might be yours, and that your joy might be complete." Notice that Jesus never says that our lives would be devoid of trouble. "In the world you will find nothing but trouble." What he does tell us is that our heart, which is the center of our existence — can retain its peace in the swirl of miseries about us just as the inner room of our home provides a tranquil haven when a severe storm is raging outside. Regardless of external circumstance, we must not let our hearts be troubled but must try to maintain a calm and trusting peace.

SATURDAY OF THE FOURTH WEEK OF EASTER
Ac 13:44-52 and Jn 14:7-14

There's a well-known text that reappears in various books of the Bible and is found in today's first reading: "I have made you a light to the nations and a means of salvation to the ends of the earth." The statement originally comes from one of the servant songs of Isaiah (49:6). It occurs again in Luke's Gospel (2:32) when Simeon accepts the baby Jesus into his arms on the occasion of the Lord's presentation in the Temple. In these two instances, it is a reference to Jesus as the Messiah. The words are not exactly the same but both speak of Jesus as being the light for all nations. That means the Messiah is not the savior of Israel alone, but he will also save the Gentiles. In the passage from the Acts of the Apostles which we heard today, Paul applies this text to the mission of the Church and to his own ministry. He says that the Lord told the apostles to be a "light to the nations." This personal conviction of his own exalted calling gives him unprecedented energy and courage. We, and all Christians, are expected to share in this sacred mission of bringing light and salvation to others. Think of this text as applying personally to you and let it be your inspiration at least for today.

MONDAY, FIFTH WEEK OF EASTER
Ac 14:5-1 and Jn 14:21-26

This is the story of a man who had never walked a day in his life until he met the Apostle Paul. He lived in the ancient town of Lystra, in the present day country of Turkey. The old town no longer exists, but its memory is still kept alive as the site of this dramatic healing. It's also the hometown of the young bishop, Timothy. Paul and Barnabas were in Lystra because they had to flee from persecution in nearby Iconium. This unfortunate circumstance in their lives proved to be a profound blessing for the crippled man. He must have been carried into the assembly where Paul was preaching and placed near the front. We have a marvelous statement made here. It says, Paul "saw he had faith to be saved." How can one see faith? It must have radiated from his heart so strongly that it registered on his face. At Paul's command, his faith enabled him to stand and take the first step he ever made. Our faith is basic to our lives. It enables us to stand up and walk. Deep faith in the death and resurrection of Jesus is the first step for us to rise higher.

TUESDAY, FIFTH WEEK OF EASTER
Ac 14:19-28 and Jn 14:27-31

The sequence of Paul's adventures continue today. Yesterday, the text explained his curing of the crippled man, which prompted the people to "worship" Barnabas and him as gods. The Jews who had forced them out of Iconium now followed them to Lystra, labeled them as charlatans, and incited the crowd to stone them. Paul was stoned till he was unconscious, dragged out of the city and left for dead. There is a powerful image here of the ministering Church. The apostles form a circle about him and pray for his recovery. In what different ways does the Church today come to the aid of fallen people? We could examine our motives and determine if we, as a believing community, do enough encircling, protecting and uplifting each other. We note that Paul was a most consistent person, who truly practiced in his personal life the same messages he preached to others. He immediately returns to the very city where he was stoned and preaches love and forgiveness. He didn't consider a law suit or worry over his violated rights. When Paul says we must undergo many trials, he says so from personal experience. This Apostle is a shining example for all dedicated people who are more concerned about accomplishing their mission than avenging their violated rights.

WEDNESDAY, FIFTH WEEK OF EASTER
Ac 15:1-6 and Jn 15:1-8

This Scripture passage highlights another of the many controversies, which erupted in the early Church between the Jews and Gentiles. Today we would term it as a disagreement between conservatives and liberals. The Jews would be called conservatives. They were, in fairness to them, trying to observe the teachings of their religion as they had been handed down through the centuries. Doctrines and practices for them were judged to be legally kosher according to their compliance to the Mosaic Law. That was their rallying cry — be faithful to the Law of Moses. The Gentiles, which often meant the Greeks, had no divine revelations, no deeply ingrained religious traditions and no knowledge or particular love of the Mosaic Law. Many times they judged more according to the intellect than the heart and acted according to common sense rather than following strict traditions. Now, when these two classes of people wanted to belong to the same newly established Church, there would be obvious differences as to what that Church should be like. Today, the Church continues to be open for all classes and all nationalities. Controversies are to be expected. Charity is expected to settle them.

THURSDAY, FIFTH WEEK OF EASTER
Ac 15:7-21 and Jn 15:9-11

Jesus always solved and settled the problems when he was with the Apostles. Now he was gone and the responsibility of finding satisfactory solutions lay squarely upon their own shoulders. They had to learn to meet with each other and discuss the many questions which presented themselves. No longer could they simply run to Jesus with their problems. Notice how the Lord had provided for this day. Peter had been earlier designated as leader and the others respected his office. They were already setting the style of Church government which would be observed in the following centuries. The Apostles were convinced that the Lord was still directing the Church through them as he had promised, although now it was being done in an invisible fashion. Here, they made a decision concerning the debated question of circumcision. All complied with the solution. It would not be required for the Gentiles. It is the nature of Church authority to be kinder, less demanding and more forgiving than civil authority. That is interpreted not as weakness but as part of the manner in which the Church is meant to function.

FRIDAY, FIFTH WEEK OF EASTER
Ac 15:22-31 and Jn 15:12-17

Couples often choose this Gospel to be read at their wedding ceremony. It expresses that tender love which we would expect to find in those planning to marry. "Love one another as I have loved you." Jesus even commands us to observe this kind of love. Those being married agree and, no doubt, strive to live in that exalted life of mutual caring. Now, reflect on this Gospel in its original context. Jesus said this not to those getting married but as a commandment for everyone to follow. Loving a spouse is one thing and loving a derelict in the gutter is another. The commandment calls us to love each other as God has loved us. Now it doesn't sound as easy and it loses some of its sweetness. The old commandment was to love your neighbor as yourself. In this new one Jesus says, "Love others as *I* have loved you." The new commandment extends the limiting word of "neighbor" to others, all others. The degree of loving is expanded from self-love to God's love for us, which is much greater than our self-love. When we appreciate the broad implications of this command, we understand the real challenge of Christian living.

SATURDAY, FIFTH WEEK OF EASTER
Ac 16:1-10 and Jn 15:18-21

This passage from Acts is filled with many fascinating bits of information. Paul is back in Lystra, where he took that terrible stoning. For most people the previous violence would have precluded any return, but, in Paul's case, it seemed to entice him to come back and conquer — with love. No doubt, the man who had received the miracle of mobility, was there to welcome him, although it is not mentioned. This time Paul meets another young citizen of Lystra, whom he invites to share the work of the ministry — Timothy. Here we are told that the Church made its first entrance into Europe by way of Macedonia. Here, too, the narrator switches from the third person to the first. Thus begins the famous "we" section. Most likely, it indicates that Luke was now traveling with Paul and his company. Many children today use the "Wee" tapes with the songs for little people. Here, in a sense, the "wee Church" was moving out into the world. Still, very young and small, it was making gigantic strides to come of age. We, too, like the infant Church may feel insignificant, but divine energy and inspiration call us to our fulfillment.

MONDAY, SIXTH WEEK OF EASTER
Ac 16:11-15 and Jn 15:26 - 16:4

These words which we read in today's Gospel were spoken at a momentous time in the life of Jesus — on the eve of his death.

He had sharply and consistently confronted the very stronghold of Pharisaism and all who promoted it. On the morrow, the Pharisees would temporarily triumph, for Jesus was finally sentenced to death. They, in their dogged adherence to the letter of the law, felt they were serving God by ridding the land of this itinerant, miracle-working troublemaker known as Jesus. In that setting we appreciate Jesus telling his disciples that they too will someday face a similar ordeal. He says, "A time will come when anyone who puts you to death will claim to be serving God." In later years when the hour came for the Apostles to accept a martyr's death, they no doubt did recall this night and these words of the Master. We may not be put to death for our belief in Jesus, but it is clearly promised that, because of Jesus and his teachings, we will face some degree of persecution. It's all very simple; living the Gospel means pain and hardship. It just goes with the territory.

TUESDAY, SIXTH WEEK OF EASTER
Ac 16:22-34 and Jn 16:5-11

Am I in prison or am I free? Physically, I'm free and able to be about, but what is my spiritual situation? Is my spirit locked in a place I would rather not be? If so, what is it that keeps me in prison and who or what is my spiritual jailor? In this passage from the Acts, Paul and Silas were beaten and thrown into prison. When they had their feet tied to a stake, this "never say no" duo began to pray and sing. Their faith shocked the prison walls and broke open the doors. They were incarcerated but actually were free. The jailer, on the other hand, was really confined to his own inner prison and the thought of killing himself seemed the only way out. Then the prisoners unlocked the chained heart of the jailer, brought light to his life and water to his dry spirit. Around the table, they all celebrated their new-found freedom. The story is one filled with inspiration and very deep meaning when applied to one's own inner life. Intervention, divine or human, still comes to free us, or make us see the situation in a more favorable light. Self destruction is never the way out. I can walk out with dignity, if I walk in the light of Christ.

WEDNESDAY, SIXTH WEEK OF EASTER
Ac 17:15, 22 - 8:1 and Jn 16:12-15

Paul did his homework well when he arrived at Athens to preach the Gospel. He climbed the hill with the flat top, around which the city was built. There, the many shrines and monuments which the Athenians held sacred, vied for his attention. One of the altars occupying the hill was dedicated: "To a God Unknown." This inscription suggested itself to Paul as the perfect opening for his impending speech. He would address the oldest and most respected council of ancient Greece in the Areopagus. It was the time and occasion, he thought, to be very intellectual and in that manner they would understand and accept the message of Jesus. The missionary Apostle was soon to learn that Athens had generated a European citizenry which was very different from those he had known in the Middle East. His carefully planned analogies from science, the poets and other intellectual sources did not move Athens to embrace Jesus. Discouraged, Paul acknowledged his presentation as one of his best speeches and poorest homilies. It was his first and final attempt at missionary intellectualizing. From here on, his preaching would boast only of Christ and Christ crucified. That message would change the face of Europe and the world.

THURSDAY, SIXTH WEEK OF EASTER
Ac 18:1-8 and Jn 16:16-20

This day is Ascension Thursday in the United States and many other countries. There are, however, some places where the Ascension is celebrated this coming Sunday — the Seventh Sunday of Easter. In those locations this passage is read today. John tells us that Jesus spoke the words in this passage on the night before he died. He mentions reappearing after a "short time," which would be a clear reference to his approaching death and soon-to-follow resurrection. Then would come the Ascension, which is an extension of the resurrection. Jesus spoke on this occasion of returning to the Father. He experienced within himself that strong yet mysterious "homeward tug" which is present in the human heart and in the instinct of so many of God's creatures. A very strong desire to return is found in the homing pigeon or the persistent salmon. They want to go back to their familiar surroundings. Many of God's creatures travel hundreds of miles and eventually find home. There was a very strong attraction within Jesus to return to his original, eternal home, which he did and which we commemorate. When death separates us from our bodies, it will be that same innate homeward tug which will pull us to our eternal home.

FRIDAY, SIXTH WEEK OF EASTER
Ac 18:9-18 and Jn 16:20-23

The poet, Francis Thompson, once wrote: "Nothing comes and nothing goes, that is not paid with moan; For we are born in another's pain and perish in our own." Jesus, facing imminent death, voices his feelings about pain and joy. He says sadness and pain in general will eventually be conquered by joy and happiness. The example of a mother giving birth to a child is presented here to demonstrate how pains become lost in joys. When a mother converses with others about her baby, she doesn't constantly discuss how painful it was to give birth. She rejoices that the child is alive and well and her attention is turned toward the future. When we are in the midst of many projects, we often must suffer in order to bring them to completion. When the project is finished, the joys of success crowd the sufferings from our minds. This section of John's Gospel offers an excellent meditation which can be used whenever we're on the verge of a difficult task. It enables us to find a proper perspective and gives us that needed faith for whatever lies ahead. It's a promise that present pains will become future joys.

SATURDAY, SIXTH WEEK OF EASTER
Ac 18:23-28 and Jn 16:23-28

Here is one of many passages in Scripture dealing with the subject of prayer. We like to take literally the words stated here but, in reality, they are not literally fulfilled in practice. We know of many requests which have been made in prayer that have not been fulfilled. People sometimes say they are "angry with God" for not answering their prayers. The more urgent and serious the request, the more angry they become. One lady said she prayed very fervently for the recovery of her friend, but he died. "Now," she said, "I'm angry with God." Two points can be made. The first is: There are no unanswered prayers. Every prayer does some good. If the prayer is answered the way we have requested, then we could not find any fault with that. If it is not, there was some good accomplished by the very fact we prayed over the matter. We are acknowledging that results may or may not happen as we want. By the very fact that we face the alternatives and vocalize them, we are better prepared to accept the results, whatever they may be. The second point is: Prayer is primarily directed to the spiritual realm which is often very nebulous. We are really pushing the point by expecting observable physical results to happen because we prayed.

MONDAY, SEVENTH WEEK OF EASTER
Ac 19:1-8 and Jn 16:29-33

The open honesty of the new converts in Ephesus is very admirable. When Paul asked them if they had received the Holy Spirit, they innocently replied, "We have not so much as heard that there is a Holy Spirit." It seems that Apollo was so enthusiastic to begin his preaching mission that he began instructing others before he, himself, had the full message. Soon, he was informed about the existence of the Holy Spirit, as also were his newly made converts. Paul simply assumes that one receives the Holy Spirit at the time of baptism. When the people said they never heard about the Spirit, he naturally inquires how they were baptized. The answer they gave was "with the baptism of John." As we are now approaching the coming Feast of Pentecost, it's an excellent time to give some thought to the coming of the Spirit into our lives. Have we truly received the Spirit into our adult lives? We are expected to live as mature, responsible Christian men and women. During this nine-day vigil, between Ascension Thursday and Pentecost Sunday, invite God's Spirit to be renewed in the depth of your being.

TUESDAY, SEVENTH WEEK OF EASTER
Ac 20:17-27 and Jn 17:1-11

Both Jesus and Paul are saying good-bye in our two readings. Jesus is doing so in his famous "priestly prayer." His thoughts are being lifted to his father, but the words are also to touch the ears and hearts of his Apostles. It's prayed just before they enter the garden, where Jesus will be arrested. About to die, he tells his Father that he had always tried to teach the truth and asks a sustaining blessing for his followers. Paul informs his followers in Miletus and Ephesus that he will be leaving them. Like Jesus, he, too, is concerned about the spiritual welfare of his converts. Paul assures them at this point that he doesn't need to revise or reverse anything he previously taught them, for he always tried to speak the truth. He always tried to tell both side of the story of Jesus — the pleasant and unpleasant. Pope John XXIII once told a portrait painter: "If you paint my face, paint it, warts and all." He didn't want to cover up or shade his true image. We are called to be honest in all circumstances. When we say something different in private than we do in public, we do a disservice to truth.

WEDNESDAY, SEVENTH WEEK OF EASTER
Ac 20:28-38 and Jn 17:11-19

Paul makes clear to the Ephesians in this passage a basic religious truth which we should also note. It is: God owns the Church. He mentions this in the context of bidding a final farewell to the pastors. They are explicitly told: "Shepherd the church of God, which he has acquired at the price of his own blood." We must never forget that the Church belongs to God. It was purchased and brought into existence at the most exorbitant price imaginable — the blood of Jesus, the Son of God. God not only owns the Church, but the Spirit of God rules the Church. Those who have donated large sums of money to the Church are certainly to be appreciated but they do not own the Church. The Church was acquired at a far greater price. It is God who speaks in the Church with an authoritative voice, who sets Church doctrines, establishes moral teachings and interprets the Scriptures. The volunteer workers don't own the Church. The pastor, bishop or pope doesn't own the Church. All are meant to be servants, nothing more. The Church is not a human institution, but a divine one, filled with humans. Thanks be to God that God's in charge.

THURSDAY, SEVENTH WEEK OF EASTER
Ac 22:30; 23:6-11 and Jn 17:20-26

This is one of the classic stories in the life and adventures of St. Paul. It shows a healthy combination of human wit and divine providence. Paul had been arrested for preaching about Jesus, which according to the Jews, was a forbidden topic. He realized that, if convicted, his prison term could be lengthy. As the charges were being read against him, he was analyzing the members of the Jewish Temple Court known as the Sanhedrin. He personally knew many of them from his former active years in Judaism. The court consisted of about seventy "judges" and Paul estimated about 30% of them were members of the Sadducee Party and 70% were Pharisees. He would use those statistics to maneuver his release. When asked to speak in his defense, Paul said he was on trial concerning the resurrection — a topic which clearly divided the two parties. This ignited an internal division in the court. He further intensified the controversy when he shouted loudly, "I'm a Pharisee." Troops had to be called in to quiet the court and, in the meantime, Paul, peacefully and unconvicted, walked away. That night, Paul says that the Lord appeared at his side and said: "Keep up your courage." So must we.

FRIDAY, SEVENTH WEEK OF EASTER
Ac 25:13-21 and Jn 21:15-19

Here is presented the very famous dialogue between Jesus and Peter. It's the last chapter of John's Gospel and Jesus is asking for a total commitment of love from the future leader of his Church. In this section, as in other parts of John's Gospel, two different Greek words are used for love — *philia* and *agape*. Philia means a close friendship. Agape is a totally selfless giving. Jesus asks, "Do you love me?" — Agape. Peter replies, "I love you." — Philia. Jesus asks a second time for agape. Peter replies with philia. Jesus, the third time, asks only for philia. Peter, for the third time, assures him of philia. Later, in his own time, Peter would make his "agape commitment" to Jesus. He would then demonstrate it with his death on a cross, as Jesus had done for him. That would be "agape par excellence." I need to often reconsider my own degree of love for Jesus. I will know my love's extent by monitoring my daily living. It's encouraging to know that Jesus is understanding and very patient — both with St. Peter and with me.

SATURDAY, SEVENTH WEEK OF EASTER
Ac 28:16-20; 30-31 and Jn 21:20-25

For the last six weeks we have been following the message of salvation through the Acts of the Apostles and the Gospel of St. John. Today we come to the conclusion of each of these outstanding books of Scripture. Fittingly, their concluding chapters center around two of the biggest names in the history of Christianity — Peter and Paul. The Acts has brought Paul to Rome, where he is under a mild "house arrest." He still can travel about with some freedom and preach of Jesus, as he awaits his trial. John's Gospel closes with Peter in Galilee, conversing with Jesus. He, too, will soon be going to Rome and there will establish the new center of the Church's mission. Peter, as the first pope of the infant Church, and Paul, as it's most outstanding missionary, will spend their last days in the Imperial City of Rome. There, both their careers will be cut short by the demented Roman Emperor,

Nero. In that city today one can view the magnificent basilicas dedicated to their honor. There, the past can be read and studied and the future envisioned, for the message moves on. Jesus is the same; yesterday, today and tomorrow.

THE FEASTS OF THE SAINTS

JANUARY 2, BASIL THE GREAT and GREGORY NAZIANZEN, BISHOPS AND DOCTORS

These two saints, Basil and Gregory, were close personal friends from the time they first met at school in Caesarea, modern day Turkey. Basil, born in 329, was one year older than Gregory and more aggressive in his personality. They came from families which were both wealthy and prominent in their social standings. Both died in their fifties, but not before they had permanently enshrined themselves in the early history of Christianity. The title, "Father of Eastern Monasticism," is applied to Basil; while Gregory is best remembered as the Archbishop of Constantinople. This feast day, honoring these two spiritual friends, can teach us the value of having a "soul partner." Such a person is not actually a spiritual director but simply someone with similar objectives in life, with whom we can share the journey. Basil and Gregory were considerably different in personality and temperament, but found each other supportive because of their common goals. Both Basil and Gregory gave their wealth to the poor and sought to find a new treasure in the desert. Through mutual support, Basil became a prolific writer on the spiritual life and Gregory, an elegant preacher and outstanding poet. Their works continue to both enlighten and inspire us as they did each other. "A faithful friend is beyond price" (Si 6:15).

JANUARY 4, ELIZABETH ANN SETON

When Betty Bailey was born in New York City in 1774, no one could have imagined the direction her life would take before it was completed at the early age of forty-seven. Her father was a physician and professor at Kings College — now known as Columbia University — and her mother was the daughter of an Episcopal priest from Staten Island, N.Y. When Elizabeth was twenty years old she married a wealthy businessman, William Seton. Within a few years they had five children. William first lost his fortune and then, his health. In an effort to relax and regain his strength, they travelled to Italy to visit the Filicchi family, who were good friends. There William died. Upon returning to the United States, Elizabeth joined the Catholic Church. For this, she was ostracized from family and many former friends. She moved first to Baltimore and then to Emmitsburg, where she founded the Sisters of Charity. Through the teaching skills of her Order, Elizabeth started the Catholic school system in this country. It was on this date, January 4, 1821, that she died at her convent in Emmitsburg, Maryland. In 1975, at the Vatican, an inspiring ceremony was held in her honor. Since then, she has had the unique distinction of being the first American-born canonized saint of the Church.

JANUARY 5, JOHN NEUMANN, BISHOP

Yesterday our liturgical attention was centered on Baltimore. Today we move 100 miles north to Philadelphia to discover another American saint — Bishop John Neumann. He was born in Bohemia in 1811 and, there, he was educated in the seminary to become a priest. He was not ordained for his native land because his diocese had enough priests. John, therefore, sailed to the United States and was ordained in New York City. He served as a parish priest in Buffalo, N.Y., and as pastor of a church in Philadelphia. Eventually he became the bishop of Philadelphia. During his eight years as bishop, he built eighty churches and the students in his Catholic schools increased twentyfold. Bishop Neumann began the Forty Hours Devotions in his diocese and it soon spread over the whole country. He had the laudable practice of visiting every parish in his diocese each year. He died on this day in 1860, as the country was preparing for the Civil War. Today Bishop John Neumann is honored as the first American bishop to be canonized a saint.

JANUARY 17, ANTHONY, ABBOT
Mt 19:16-26

Our saint today is Anthony of Egypt, born in 250 A.D. and famous for his asceticism in the Egyptian desert. He is not to be confused with Anthony of Padua, who lived nearly a thousand years later. Anthony of Egypt, known as "The Abbot," was born with a temperament which indicated his life's direction. He was a very private person. He found school distasteful and avoided other children. The parish church offered him both a social haven and a classroom of spiritual study. The Gospel he heard in church became his teacher. Following the death of his wealthy parents, Anthony provided enough money for his younger sister and donated the remainder to the poor. For a time he was instructed by an elderly hermit, whom he had befriended. Solitude, then, called him to live in an empty tomb and eventually invited him to the desert. Complete seclusion eluded Anthony for, as in the case of Jesus, the crowds followed and sought him for his wisdom. Now, tempered by asceticism, he returned to society to speak and minister. Later, however, the inner call to blessed solitude enticed him back to the desert, and there he lived until the age of 105. Anthony teaches that we all must follow the call of God within and walk to the rhythm of our own heartbeats.

JANUARY 21, AGNES, VIRGIN AND MARTYR

We may at times be very critical of young people and think of them as irresponsible and selfish. Today the Church honors a very young girl about thirteen years of age who loved Jesus so much that she preferred to die a martyr's death rather than offend her Lord. Tradition says that St. Agnes lived in Rome around 300 A.D. and was popular because of her outstanding beauty. Her innocent conduct of life called even more attention to her and this led to her being reported to the authorities as a Christian, which in her day was still forbidden. Several attempts were made to pressure her to renounce her loyalty to Jesus, all to no avail. It was then she was faced with execution, which she accepted. Such a resolute conviction in anyone would be admirable, but especially in a mere child of thirteen. It was with Christian courage that she gave her life to the Lord in the painful death of martyrdom. Agnes is often pictured holding a lamb in her arms as a symbol that she, too, was a lamb of God, obedient to her shepherd. The Latin word for lamb is *"agnus"* and that is the derivation of the name Agnes. Many times, the old teach the young and sometimes the young teach the old. Today Agnes teaches us all about conviction, pain and love.

JANUARY 24, FRANCIS DE SALES, BISHOP AND DOCTOR

This seventeenth-century holy man had a particular talent for making people interested in the spiritual life and directing their journey to God. He was educated in Paris, France and later received a doctorate in law at Padua, Italy. He then studied for the priesthood and was ordained in 1593. Nine years later Francis was named bishop of Geneva, Switzerland, where he brought back to the Church more than 70,000 who had drifted away. It was his spiritual direction which guided another very holy person,

St. Jane Frances de Chantal. Together, they founded the Visitation Order of Sisters which is dedicated to teaching and care of the sick. Francis spent a considerable amount of his time writing pamphlets and books for those who wished to be instructed in the faith. His *Treatise on the Love of God*, was written for the Sisters in the Visitation Order. His second classic, *Introduction to a Devout Life*, written for lay people, became, for many years, required reading for every aspirant to the priesthood. Today, we honor this sensitive, seventeenth-century saint, who has helped the world to know and love Jesus. Francis has left us many oft-repeated sayings. Two are: "More flies are caught with a spoonful of honey than with a hundred barrels of vinegar." "If one must err, let it be on the side of gentleness."

JANUARY 25, CONVERSION OF PAUL, APOSTLE
Ac 22:3-16 or Ac 9:1-22 and Mk 16:15-18

The term "conversion," literally means to "turn with." In a very dramatic way, Paul turns to go with the teachings of Jesus as his new mentor, as opposed to the Old Testament Law. This famous "on the road experience" is a type of death-resurrection sequence. He is stopped and literally knocked to the ground. The light has disappeared from his eyes, as a symbol of death. Lying in the dust is a reminder of the grave. Saul, with all his religious fervor for the Old Law, has now "died." The Risen Lord, who had recently returned from the dead, calls forth from the dust the Apostle who, from this time on will be known as Paul. Now all his zealous energy, previously employed to destroy the Church, is redirected toward its survival. The conversion of this dynamic and energetic missionary will be a tremendous boost of morale for the fledging Christian Church. The event was so important that Luke tells it, in detail, three times in the Acts of the Apostles. It would be liturgically fitting today to recall some type of death-resurrection experience in our own lives. Maybe we would want to tell it to another. Should we choose to do so, it would be a kind of witness preaching, something that Paul did frequently and effectively.

JANUARY 26, TIMOTHY and TITUS, BISHOPS
2 Tm 1:1-8 or Tt 1:1-5

There was considerable speculation in the first century that the world would soon end. The selection of Timothy and Titus as successors of the original twelve Apostles, told the people that the Church believed the world would continue. This "second generation" of apostles would lead the Church into future centuries, into new missionary territories and into unfathomable depths of personal faith awareness. Both of these young men were recruited into the ministry by Paul. He personally offered them directions and sent both on several assignments. Sometimes they travelled with him. Timothy was in charge of the church in Corinth for a time and was replaced by Titus, who exercised more discipline. Timothy was a timid person, as noted in 1 Cor 16:10. Paul also shows sensitivity to his needs in his second letter to Timothy (1:7). Tradition says he died a martyr's death. Titus was much bolder and served as Paul's trouble shooter. Paul left him on the Island of Crete then wrote to him: "Cretans have ever been liars, beasts and lazy gluttons, and that's the simple truth" (1 Tt 1:12). Had Timothy been assigned to Crete, he would have been "eaten alive," but not Titus. He soon put them all in line. In his epistles to Timothy, Paul is supportive and encouraging, a quality missing in his letter to Titus. Yet it is very evident that Paul has a far deeper trust in Titus' ability.

JANUARY 28. THOMAS AQUINAS, PRIEST AND DOCTOR

The life of Thomas (1225 - 1274) is perfectly framed in the center of the famous thirteenth century. Although he was allotted only forty-nine years, they were choice years. Faithful to his namesake, Thomas the Apostle, Aquinas questioned most everything and sought an answer for it. He recorded his intellectual and faith-centered insights to assist others. So keen was his mental acumen and so enlightening his teaching, that his views often carried as much weight as the Bible. Frequently, scholars on opposing sides of a vexing theological question, would each quote Thomas to support their positions. This native born Italian saint is best known for his famous *Summa Theologica* which has continued to be a guiding light for over 700 years. There, one can see his ability to treat complicated subjects in a simple and understandable manner. His definition of law is a good example. "Law," he says, "is an ordinance of reason for the common good, made by the person who has care of the community." Besides his deep theological writings, Thomas composed such well known Latin hymns as: "Pange Lingua," "Tantum Ergo," "Panis Angelicus," "O Salutaris Hostia" and others. Likewise, he left us prayers and spiritual poems, plus many commentaries on books of Scripture for our spiritual meditation and development.

JANUARY 31. JOHN BOSCO, PRIEST

John Bosco was born in Turin, Italy, in 1815. Two years later his father died. This future saint, raised by his mother, experienced the pains of poverty at a very tender age. John's life work was inspired by these early years. He wanted to become a priest, specifically to assist youth. Ordained at the age of twenty-six, John — commonly called Don (Father) Bosco — immediately began his work with orphans. Soon, he opened a hospice for boys and his mother served as the housekeeper. Within a short time, 150 homeless boys who were living there were instructed in religion and given opportunities to learn skills. Workshops for tailoring, shoemaking and printing were available. Don Bosco trained his own staff to assist in the care of the youth. They organized under the patronage of St. Francis de Sales and, eventually, became a religious congregation known as the Salesians. They were dedicated to the care of orphans and other boys and girls who were homeless. The mission spread rapidly from northern Italy to the entire country. When Don Bosco died in 1888, the congregation was only twenty years old, but it numbered over 1000 members. It had spread to seven countries in Europe and South America. Don Bosco insisted on the positive values of formation for youth and rejected corporal punishment. He, a pioneer of vocational training, continues to be an inspiration for all who have a dream of helping disadvantaged youth.

FEBRUARY 2, PRESENTATION OF THE LORD
Ml 3:1-4; Heb 2:14-18 and Lk 2:22-40

It was an old Jewish custom for parents to take their newborn children to the temple and present them to their God. The ritual was accomplished either forty or eighty days after birth. The Feast of the Presentation of Jesus is, therefore, celebrated in the Church on February 2 each year — forty days after Christmas. Gray-haired Simeon and aging Anna were waiting in the temple to welcome Jesus. Luke says they were present every day. They felt "at home" in the temple as they prayed and waited to see Jesus. Many days they had come, but this was the day for which they had been waiting. Imagine Mary holding Jesus and then placing him into the arms of Simeon. It was on this occasion that Mary and Joseph learned from Simeon that Jesus would be a future source of controversy. Both of them, likewise, would be subjected to many trials because of their close relationship to Jesus. We even get a brief glimpse into the soul of Simeon, who says he's now ready to die because he has seen the Messiah. Simeon and Anna accepted Jesus. They became pioneer Jewish Christians. They had both received sacred communications from the Holy Spirit and holy communion and now are perfectly content to die. Jesus had fulfilled their lives and promises to be their complete fulfillment on the other side of death.

FEBRUARY 5, AGATHA

History identifies the Roman Emperor who reigned between 249-251 A.D. as the Yugoslavian, Decius. It was his desire to see the ancient religious traditions once again observed in Rome. Every citizen was to pass a "loyalty test" by offering worship to the Roman gods. The immediate result was a renewed persecution against those Christians who refused to comply. Certificates were given to all who offered their sacrifices as proof of their allegiance. It is said that a number of Christians did sacrifice to the gods and, thereby, compromised their faith. Others refused and, as a result, suffered persecution and death. Among those who died under Decius was the Pope — Fabian. Another, according to tradition, was Agatha — a young, beautiful Sicilian lady. Speculation only can suggest the exact nature of her ordeal, but several accounts witness to the fact of her willingness to die, rather than bow to this pagan pressure. Her Church says, "thanks for the witness," and continues to keep alive her memory, on this, her feast day.

FEBRUARY 6, PAUL MIKI AND COMPANIONS, MARTYRS
Gal 2:19-20 and Mt 28:16-20

When we hear an account of a group of people being killed at Nagasaki, Japan, undoubtedly, most of us would think of those who suffered death from the Atomic bomb on August 9, 1945. The average estimates of those who died from the original blast and the following radiation are about 55,000. Today, though, the Church remembers another, lesser known, group of twenty-six people who died there nearly 350 years before the dropping of the bomb. They were Jesuits, Franciscans and laypeople of Japanese and European nationalities. Their deaths were not the result of a military encounter, but of the fact that they were ambassadors of peace. Paul Miki, a Jesuit brother, was the leading spokesman for the group on the momentous, last day in their lives. His name, therefore, heads and identifies the group. Their deaths by crucifixion were both politically and religiously motivated. One would not have imagined that crucifixion was still a reality in the world at the beginning of the seventeenth century. We give these saints our honored remembrance for they, like Jesus, "humbled themselves, obediently accepting even death, death on a cross" (Ph 2:8) for the sake of the faith they loved.

FEBRUARY 10, SCHOLASTICA, VIRGIN

Among the many notable facts in the life of St. Scholastica is that she had a famous twin brother — St. Benedict. Born in Nursia, Italy, in 480, this brother and sister founded the Order of Benedictine monks and sisters respectively. Both branches today are still active and functioning according to their originally established guidelines. The fifth century was an ideal time for the rapid expansion of the Church, for now Christianity was the official religion in the Roman Empire. In 380, the Roman Emperor, Theodocius, had not only declared Christianity the State religion, but the worship of the old pagan gods was also forbidden. The Roman Empire had done a complete about-face and the Church was the benefactor. The Benedictines were the first in the west to establish an Order of men and women. Scholastica guided her branch of the Order and applied to it many of the teachings of her brother. Much of the information we have about Scholastica comes from the writings of St. Gregory the Great, who became pope about forty years after her death. He notes in his *Dialogues* that Benedict knew of his sister's death, although he was not present. He saw "her soul leaving her body in the form of a dove."

FEBRUARY 14, CYRIL, MONK and METHODIUS, BISHOP

Paul wrote two letters to those living in the Greek city of Thessalonica. It would be expected that the Christians of that city would read and memorize those letters for generations to follow. They warn of many hardships in living the faith and making Christ known to others. Cyril and his brother Methodius were born in Thessalonica and heard those words often. There were seven children in their family and Cyril was the youngest. However, Methodius outlived his younger brother by sixteen years. They had early contact with Slavic speaking people due to their father's job. They learned their language and, thereby, were directed to their future missions. Both were well educated and ordained to the ministry. Their lives became immersed in the struggle for religious and political freedom for the Slavic people. They introduced Slavic translations of the Bible as well as other liturgical books to be used in the liturgy. Hostility erupted from those who insisted the language must be Hebrew, Greek or Latin. This was only one of their many struggles to bring the ninth century Slavic people to a better understanding of Jesus. Cyril died in Rome at the age of forty-two. Methodius lived for sixteen years more and died in the year 884.

FEBRUARY 22, CHAIR OF PETER, APOSTLE
1 P 5:1-4 and Mt 16:13-19

Our liturgy this day does not revolve around a piece of

furniture as the title might suggest, it rather draws attention to the position of leadership in the Church. Peter was designated by Jesus to be the "chairman of the board." The term, chair, refers to the seat of power and the place from where an organization is controlled. In federal government we often hear such phrases as, "The chair recognizes the senator from New York." Universities have their various chairs of philosophy, science, English, etc. The term comes from the Latin, "cathedra" which means seat or chair. Thus the cathedral is the church where the chair of the bishop is located. The same concept is carried into the parish church, where the chair of the one who presides at the liturgy is located in a very visible place. Note also that the term, chair, designates a seat for one person only, as opposed to a bench or pew. The Pope's chair in Rome is a visible sign of papal leadership. It commemorates the more than 260 popes who have followed Peter in that exalted office.

FEBRUARY 23, POLYCARP, BISHOP AND MARTYR
Rv 2:8-11

Polycarp is a distinctive Greek name meaning, "much fruit." As a productive tree, he was an inspiration to his contemporaries and has greatly benefitted historians of succeeding generations. Polycarp served the Church in a unique way, being a very important link between John, the last of the Apostles and Irenaeus, one of the early Fathers of the Church. The sequence is, John, a disciple of Jesus, died about 100. Polycarp, a disciple of John, died around 165. Irenaeus, a disciple of Polycarp, died in 202. The teachings of Jesus were, thus, conveyed directly and accurately into the beginning of the 3rd century. Polycarp is a key bridge of communication. He faithfully recorded the past and was a reliable witness for the future. It is said that this energetic bishop of Smyrna was martyred by fire in the city's local stadium at the age of 86. And it is further reported that the calmness with which he accepted martyrdom left a lasting impression on his local congregation. His life and works, as his name suggests, still produce many fruitful blessings for us today.

MARCH 7. PERPETUA and FELICITY, MARTYRS

Various combinations of saintly people have been united under a single feast day. There are young bishops — Timothy and Titus; brothers — Cyril and Methodius; and apostles — Philip and James. Today's feast brings together yet another unique pair. Perpetua was a distinguished lady of Carthage and Felicity was her slave. These two names highlight this feast but the account of their martyrdom says others died at the same time. Many of the ordeals they endured in prison were recorded by Perpetua and have been preserved. At the time of their deaths, Perpetua had a dependent baby boy and Felicity died only three days after giving birth to a daughter. These circumstances and other details of their lives caused them to be highly honored by the other Christians at that time. They died in Carthage in 202. Tertullian, the outstanding Church historian of the period, verifies these happenings. He says they left their cells and walked to their deaths with peaceful looks and showed no fear.

MARCH 17. PATRICK, BISHOP

On the third day of creation God said, "Let the dry land appear." And so it did. He called the dry land earth. An old legend continues the story. God touched the earth with his finger and left his trademark. The spot he touched is now known as Ireland. From that blessed touch shamrocks sprang forth. Their threefold leaves tell of the nature of their Maker and also commemorate the third day on which the earth was created. The first man and woman were Irish, so the legend continues. The original paradise was Ireland. This is unknown to most people but Scripture seems to affirm the fact. The "evidence" is that after Adam and Eve had sinned they covered themselves, not with fig leaves as some would have us believe, but with shamrocks. Ireland is the only land that grows shamrocks large enough for that purpose. It's most unfortunate the original couple did not possess the qualities of their famous descendant, Patrick. Had they been so blessed, they would have driven the tempting snake out of paradise and spared the human race much misery. We honor Patrick today as a bishop of the Church and a man of deep faith. Like all saints, he is for all people and all times. St. Patrick and March 17th makes us think of the past and smile at the many "rich stories of our faith."

MARCH 19, JOSEPH, HUSBAND OF MARY
2 S 7:4-5, 12-14, 16; Rm 4:13, 16-18, 22 and Mt 1:16, 18-21, 24 or Lk 2:41-51

The Scriptures highlight two famous men by the name of Joseph. One was a patriarch in the first book of the Old Testament who saved his people from starvation. The other was the husband of Mary and guardian of the child Jesus. A divine mission took each of them from Israel to Egypt and both their fathers were named Jacob. The husband of Mary is like the patriarch of old reappearing after eighteen centuries and tracing his ancestry through King David who was a native of Bethlehem. It was the Roman census which brought Mary and Joseph from Nazareth to Bethlehem, Joseph's ancestral home. They had come to register as the law required, and then, because of Herod's plot on the life of the child Jesus, they fled to Egypt. When the Holy Family returned from Egypt, they could probably have settled in Bethlehem. However, fearing further persecution by Archelaus, they went back north to Nazareth where Jesus grew up. The last we hear of Joseph in the Scriptures is when Jesus is twelve years old and they find him in the temple. Mary tells Jesus, "Your father and I have been looking for you with great anxiety." We show special devotion to Joseph because of the precious sanctity of his life and his unique role in the early days of Jesus. We express our love and respect for him in our celebration of this feast day.

MARCH 25, THE ANNUNCIATION OF OUR LORD
Is 7:10-14; Heb 10:4-10 and Lk 1:26-38

We celebrate our birthdays but not the days on which we were conceived, for we probably don't know those exact days. Today's feast is a commemoration of the conception of Jesus in Mary's womb. This first flicker of human life would eventually become the Savior of the World. Did Mary understand all that she was consenting to? Most likely not. Did she realize this was God? Most likely not. Did she truly put flesh on the invisible God so we could see him? Yes. Mary began today to prepare for us the Way, the Truth and the Life. Jesus bestowed incredible dignity on the people of this earth by his willingness to become human. This day causes us to think of our origins: how and when we came to be. Were we wanted and planned for? Who was the first person your mother told that she was pregnant with you? In which season of the year were you conceived and what were some of the events that happened in your mother's life when she carried you? Mary began her pregnancy with a strenuous journey to Elizabeth. There must have followed long quiet days of prayer and thought about her developing baby. Finally there came the long trip to Bethlehem and those precious events of the first Christmas. This is an excellent day to pray the Angelus, in honor of Mary, and to offer a heartfelt prayer for our own mothers.

APRIL 7, JOHN BAPTIST DE LA SALLE, PRIEST

La Salle College in Philadelphia is but one of many reminders of the energetic and saintly man, John Baptist de la Salle. John was born in Reims, France in 1651, the eldest son of an aristocratic family. He studied in fine schools including the Sorbonne and the Seminary of Saint Sulpice, where he was ordained. To help the poor boys of seventeenth-century France, he opened a charity school and this led him on his life's work. John's main concern was the recruitment and further training of good teachers. The teachers began to live together for mutual encouragement and to develop a disciplined way of life. This eventually lead to the establishment of the Brothers of the Christian Schools. La Salle emphasized the Christian aspect of education. The boys had one-half hour of Christian instruction each day and one and a half hours on Sunday. John began to receive numerous requests for the services of his teaching Brothers and soon they spread throughout France. La Salle died on Good Friday, 1719. He was canonized in 1900 and is now declared the patron of all teachers.

APRIL 11, STANISLAUS, BISHOP AND MARTYR

Today we honor a Catholic bishop who is the patron saint of Poland. He freely gave his life and blood to the Church and to his country, both of which he deeply loved. In 1072, Stanislaus became the bishop of Krakow. He had received an excellent education and possessed a seasoned reputation for being a deeply spiritual leader. At this time the Polish people were in opposition to their King, Boleslaus, because of his prolonged military expeditions. The King's own brother, Ladislaus, led a faction against the King and Stanislaus joined the cause. Infuriated by the bishop's opposition, it is said that King Boleslaus personally killed him in the church of St. Michael in Krakow. There are conflicting reports as to the exact motive of the King's hatred of Stanislaus. Some say it was because the bishop had condemned Boleslaus for kidnapping the wife of a nobleman and taking her to his castle. The killing of Stanislaus also "killed" any further political hope for Boleslaus. To save his life, the King fled to Hungary, spending his remaining years in a monastery. The cathedral in Krakow was renamed in honor of Stanislaus and here his body is buried.

APRIL 25, MARK, EVANGELIST
1 P 5:5-14 and Mk 16:15-20

St. Mark is not one of the original Twelve Apostles but he was a contemporary and was extensively involved in the life of the first-century Church. Mark, sometimes called John Mark, was a traveling companion of Paul and Barnabas. On the first missionary trip, Mark left them and returned to Jerusalem where his mother, Mary, owned a house. This well known incident of his departure caused a rift between Paul and Barnabas. Barnabas, who was Mark's cousin, wanted to take him on another journey but Paul refused. The result was that Barnabas and Mark began to travel as a team, while Paul began traveling with Silas (Ac 15:39-40). Mark was also a close friend of Peter. His Gospel, in fact, is based on the preaching of Peter. It is the shortest of the four Gospels and the most vivid. Mark quickly and, with scant introduction, bounces from one scene and subject to another. From him, we get the impression that Jesus was practically racing through his ministry. Tradition relates that Mark became bishop of Alexandria in Egypt. His relics are buried in Venice, Italy, and the world famous St. Mark's Cathedral is one of the city's most impressive highlights.

APRIL 29, CATHERINE OF SIENA, VIRGIN
1 Jn 1:5 - 2:2

It's amazing to note that Catherine, a twin, was the youngest of twenty-three children. It is even more difficult to grasp the fact that she accomplished so many deeds of national and international proportions and yet died at the early age of thirty-three. With only "a few" years to live, she matured quickly and, at the age of seven, showed a loudly-heralded attraction for the spiritual life. As a young lady, she formed about her a group of holy and highly intellectual people. Two major political interests inspired her: one involved the Crusades. She wanted the Turks to leave the Holy Land. The second involved the Papacy. She wanted the popes to leave their seventy-year residency in Avignon, France and return to Rome. The success of the Crusades is debatable, but the popes did return to the Eternal City in 1378, two years before she died. Catherine was known as a Christ-centered mystic and one of the most influential people of the fourteenth century. Her spirituality was based on such notables as Augustine, Bernard and Thomas Aquinas. In 1937, Catherine of Siena and Francis of Assisi were declared the patron saints of Italy.

MAY 1, ST. JOSEPH, WORKER
Gn 1:26 - 2:3 or Col 3:14-15, 17, 23-34 and Mt 13:54-58

Joseph is much more than a worker. He is a true man. In today's society, there are many mixed views as to what a real man actually is. Some think you must be a strong macho type of individual to be a genuine man. Joseph wasn't that type. At Jerusalem there was no room in the inn and Joseph didn't demand one. Was that weakness or manliness? He was married to the world's most beautiful woman and did not have sex. Did that make him less or more of a man? Quote some statement Joseph made or even one word. You can't. There is nothing recorded in the pages of Sacred Scripture which is spoken by Joseph. Some think to be a man one must be boisterous and ribald in conversation, and be entertaining. That would contrast sharply with the peaceful silence which probably characterized the home of Joseph and Mary in Nazareth. When the interior life of a person is tranquil, one can hear God speaking much more clearly. How important it is for us to ponder, as Mary did, and quietly meditate, like Joseph, about our callings, our duties and our lives in the presence of God. When Jesus is in your home and heart, you don't need to talk but rather listen. I wonder if Jesus, himself, learned to accept rejection, practice self-denial and hold his tongue in disciplined silence from the example of his foster father. Joseph was a peaceful, quiet and strong man. He attracted God's attention and is forever blessed.

MAY 2, ATHANASIUS, BISHOP
1 Jn 5:1-5 and Mt 10:22-25

Our saint today comes from that thriving city of Alexandria, in the northeast corner of Egypt. There, Athanasius was born in 295 A.D., and there he died seventy-eight years later. The son of a Christian family and the recipient of a classical education, Athanasius entered the ranks of the clergy at an early age. He attended the famous First Council of Nicea, but at the time he was still relatively unknown. Athanasius was lifted into the limelight at the age of thirty-three when he was made bishop of Alexandria. Many of his episcopal difficulties were caused by Arius, a fellow Alexandrian priest. Arius and his followers found fault with the Church's teaching of the divinity of Christ. The strength and political clout of the Arians forced Athanasius into exile a number of times. He is also remembered for his dogmatic writings, which were mainly discourses against the Arians and in support of the

Nicene creed. He, therefore, notes many of the Trinitarian and Christological debates of his day. The Athanasian Creed still exists, proclaiming the Christian faith in forty rhythmical phrases.

MAY 3, PHILIP and JAMES, APOSTLES
1 Cor 15:1-8 and Jn 14:6-14

Philip was from Bethsaida, the fishing village where two other apostles, Andrew and Peter, kept their boats. Philip invited his best friend, Nathanael, to meet Jesus. When Nathanael skeptically asked, "Can anything good come out of Nazareth?" Philip convinced him with three words, "Come and see." Nathanael saw and stayed. Later in the Gospel story, some Gentiles approached Philip with the request, "Sir, we wish to see Jesus." It was another perfect occasion to say, "Come and see." James, who shares this feast day with Philip, is often referred to as the younger or the lesser to distinguish him from the other apostle James. He became the first bishop of Jerusalem — an extremely important position, especially in the early Church, before the move to Rome. He is the author of one epistle, which bears his name. In it, the follower of Jesus is constantly encouraged to accomplish good works. This unique apostle and author was most likely a first cousin of Jesus. Today we walk for a moment in the memory of these two apostles who have left their indelible footprints in the sands of time.

MAY 14, MATTHIAS, APOSTLE
Ac 1:15-17, 20-26 and Jn 15:9-17

Matthias is the apostle who was selected by the Eleven to fulfill the unexpired term of Judas. Nothing is heard of him in Scripture prior to the election ceremony. After the choice is made, the Bible never mentions him again. He was not a headline person. In the Church there is a need for the quiet and passive as well as the bold and aggressive. Speaking out with confident faith is one way to witness to Christ but there are other ways. We can give witness by the things we don't say. We can demonstrate patience, humility, thoughtfulness and numerous qualities in a variety of ways. What a headline story it would have been if Paul had been chosen for this position instead of Matthias. We would have said that the Holy Spirit directed the election. We still believe the Holy Spirit guided the election and Paul was not chosen. Matthias was a type of "footnote person" and he simply was himself. That's the type the Lord wanted. There was obviously that quiet side to Jesus also. He lived those long silent years. So what can we say of Matthias? He was a true disciple of Jesus. Can that be said of us?

MAY 26. PHILIP NERI. PRIEST

Philip was born in Florence in 1515 into a prosperous family. He by-passed a business career to give his life entirely to God. After pursuing his studies, which were leading him to ordination, he abandoned them. For the next thirteen years, Philip went his own unique way, living as a spiritual nomad. In these years, Philip became "street wise," growing in his understanding of this way of life and a deeper appreciation of the people who lived it. Part of his efforts, during this time, went toward organizing leaders to assist the poor. Convinced by a friend that he could better lead this work as a priest, he was ordained at age thirty-six. He continued his association with the poor. They were invited to join in church services, picnics, musical events, and gala processions to visit other sanctuaries. Twice, Philip was reported to the pope, who in turn asked him to desist certain practices which were thought to be more carnival than religious. On both occasions, he was soon permitted to continue. The list of those who came to visit him and seek spiritual direction reads like a sixteenth-century "Who's Who in Roman Catholicism." There was Ignatius of Loyola, Camillus de Lellis, Charles Borromeo, Francis de Sales, etc. Today we re-visit this jovial and caring saint who so loved life and people.

MEMORIAL DAY

Today is a civil holiday on which we remember those who have died. It originally began to be observed after the Civil War by Southern women, when they would decorate the graves of veterans on May 30. The date was most likely chosen by Cassandra Moncure who was of French origin and lived in Virginia. It is assumed that she selected this date because May 30 in France was known as "The Day of Ashes." That was the day the ashes of Napoleon were buried in France after they had been exhumed from the Island of St. Helena. Eventually, the observance was extended to honor the dead of all wars and then to the deceased in general. Today we decorate the graves with flags and flowers. In some areas of our country along the seashores, tiny ships filled with flowers are set adrift to honor those who died at sea. In this pleasant season of the year, just before summer, we renew our appreciation for all who made our country a loving place of freedom. Each Mass we say is also a memorial of the death and resurrection of Jesus. It is to the eternal God we commend our beloved dead at this Mass. May they be at peace now and forevermore.

MAY 31.   VISITATION
Zp 3:14-18 or Rm 12:9-16 and Lk 1:39-56

Mary's visit to Elizabeth shows the extraordinary sensitivity of the Mother of Jesus. She had just spoken to an angel and consented to become the mother of Jesus. What an honor and dignity God had conferred upon her. Imagine receiving an outstanding award or promotion and, instead of sharing it with others, leaving town for three months to help a relative. That's precisely what Mary did. She simply ignored herself and immediately began a one-hundred-mile journey of mercy. Only after she arrived and established herself in the home of Elizabeth did she begin to think of her own blessings. Then she poured out her heart in a hymn of loving praise and thanksgiving. Here we are made privy to the unique love between God and Mary. It was the presence of Jesus within that made her reach out immediately, offering a service to her cousin and a song to her God. Her visitation song — the Magnificat — is positive and joy-filled. It expresses no sorrow and contains no petitions, for there was nothing more that she wanted. If I am inwardly at peace, I, too, can better face the long journey of life and sing a happy song along the way.

JUNE. SACRED HEART
A: Mt 11:25-30; B: Jn 19:31-37; C: Lk 15:3-7

One of our most familiar symbols of love is that of the heart. It appears everywhere and often on bumper stickers it is used to say, "love," rather than printing out the word. Physically, the heart is a muscle; spiritually, it is a symbol. A reference to the heart is a way of referring to the total interior life of a person. Since no heart has loved more than the heart of Jesus, his heart is sacred par excellence. The many artistic paintings of the Sacred Heart and our frequent references may cause some to consider the Sacred Heart as a kind of divine person in itself. The Sacred Heart is simply another image or symbol of Jesus. It is Jesus, viewed from the perspective of his tremendous love for us. When we honor Jesus under the symbol of the Sacred Heart, we are expressing awe and offering praise and thanksgiving for all that Jesus is and for all the love the Savior shares with us. When we give our love to God, we are having a heart-to-heart talk.

JUNE 1. JUSTIN. MARTYR
1 Cor 1:18-25

Whenever we mention the name Justin, we add, almost automatically, the word, martyr. Many saints are martyrs but we often are not aware of it. In the case of Justin, we can't forget it. He is remembered as one of the outstanding Christian personalities of the second century. He was born in Israel of Greek parents, in what is today the West Bank area. He possessed an insatiable desire to learn the truth, wherever he could find it. This led him to study the works of his famous Greek ancestors — Socrates, Plato and Aristotle. He also tells us that he held several conversations with some elderly Christian person down by the lake side. There he learned of Jesus and many of the Old Testament people of faith, especially Abraham. It is reported that Justin had a deep admiration for the martyrs. He was fascinated that they believed in a person and a cause so much that they were willing to die rather than deny. We find in Justin a rare combination of faith and reason and, being a writer, he was able to formulate his beliefs making use of both. While teaching school in Rome, he was arrested. When asked if he were a Christian, he emphatically replied: "Yes, I am a Christian." Then he started teaching the court about Jesus. He died in 165 A.D.

JUNE 3. CHARLES LWANGA and COMPANIONS. MARTYRS

The liturgy draws our attention today to Uganda, one of the smaller countries among the fifteen which comprise Central Africa. Lying due north of the famous Lake Victoria, Uganda professes as its major religions: Christianity, Islam and Tribal Religions. It was here that Charles Lwanga was born in 1860. Here, also he died, twenty-six years later. Today, he and twenty-one of his companions are honored as saints of the Church since their canonization in 1964. Charles served in the royal household of the king and was baptized there at the age of twenty-five. The king, it is reported, was "using" the young men in the court for his personal homosexual desires. Charles attempted to warn them and shield them from the king. He organized the young men, gave them instructions in religion and baptized them. Together, they professed their faith and refused to cooperate with the king. They were arrested after making a public profession of faith. All twenty-two were martyred, but Charles was singled out for an especially cruel death by fire. Pius XI declared him patron of youth for tropical Africa.

JUNE 5. BONIFACE, BISHOP AND MARTYR

Boniface is remembered as the archbishop of Mainz and the apostle of Germany. Like so many patron saints of countries, Boniface was not a native. He was born in England about 675 A.D. and was called Winfrid. Only later did he take the name Boniface. He became a member of the Benedictine Order and was distinguished for his love of learning and gifts as an orator. When he was about forty, Boniface seriously began his missionary activities. At the time he was the abbot of his monastery but he resigned that position in order to give his time and efforts to the missions. Several trips to Rome and frequent consultations with the pope set him on his way to Germany with the Church's blessings. Pope Gregory III was the one who especially encouraged Boniface to organize the German Church. The pope supported him with letters to the bishops who were already working in that country. Boniface exerted much energy in Bavaria by organizing dioceses and conducting the first Bavarian Synod in 740. He also gave five years of his life to bring needed reforms to the Frankish Church. He and fifty-three companions were martyred at Fulda (about 150 miles northeast of Frankfurt). Fulda became famous as a place of pilgrimage to honor St. Boniface.

JUNE 11. BARNABAS, APOSTLE
Ac 11:21-26; 13:1-3 and Mt 10:7-13

Today's feast upholds a prominent member of the early Church in Jerusalem. His name and deeds are well documented in the pages of Scripture. Born on the Island of Cyprus of Greek parentage, Barnabas was a contemporary of Jesus. He found his way to Palestine and was most likely numbered among the seventy-two disciples of the Lord. The Acts of the Apostles (4:36-37) recounts how Barnabas sold his farm and donated all the money to the Church. The same passage also says he was first called Joseph, but his name was changed to Barnabas, meaning "son of encouragement." Perhaps one of the most significant deeds of Barnabas was to find Paul after his conversion on the road to Damascus and encourage him to begin preaching. Paul had been rejected by the Apostles either out of fear or anger and not accepted into the ministry. The whole history of the Church would have been very different if this "Son of Encouragement" had not brought that needed encouragement to Paul. They joined in many missionary labors together. Later Barnabas and Mark traveled to Cyprus. It is said that Barnabas died a martyr's death in his own homeland of Cyprus.

JUNE 13. ANTHONY OF PADUA. PRIEST AND DOCTOR

Anthony, the beloved saint of Italy, was not Italian. He was Portuguese, born in Lisbon, Portugal about the year 1195. He died thirty-five years later near Padua, Italy, with a reputation as an effective intercessor, which time only continues to augment. Anthony entered the Franciscan monastery and soon became an expert in Sacred Scripture. He was inspired by the Franciscan martyrs in Morocco and requested to go there. Poor health forced him to leave Morocco to return to Portugal but his ship was driven to Sicily. From there he went to preach in Northern Italy and Southern France. St. Francis of Assisi personally appointed Anthony the first professor of theology for the Franciscan Friars. He spent the final three years of his life in Italy. During the Lenten season in 1231 Anthony preached daily in Padua. His delicate health was unable to support this extraordinary work load and Anthony died later that year. Anthony has been invoked as the patron saint of many causes. "Finder of Lost Objects" often heads the list. His personal life and Christian teachings have helped many find Jesus.

JUNE 21. ALOYSIUS GONZAGA. RELIGIOUS

The saint, whose life we remember today, lived only twenty-three years. He was born in northern Italy, near Mantua, only five years after the closing of the Council of Trent. It was a time of turmoil in both Church and state alike. He was raised amidst violence which saw the murders of two of his brothers. Aloysius rebelled against the military life which his father had envisioned for him and followed in the ways of his devout mother. Aloysius joined the Society of Jesus, much to his father's dislike. This struggle caused him to renounce his father's inheritance. Even though his young life was pressured by the hate and violence around him, he also had close contact with saintly people. He had received his First Communion from St. Charles Borromeo and his spiritual director at college was St. Robert Bellarmine. His short life was given almost entirely to his spiritual development. Very early on he manifested an avid desire for meditation, prayer and kindly service to others. While caring for the sick in Rome during an epidemic, he contracted a disease and died. Aloysius was canonized in 1726 and declared patron of youth.

JUNE 24. BIRTH OF JOHN THE BAPTIST
Vigil: Lk 1:5-17; Day: Lk 1:57-66, 80

John, immediately preceded Jesus and bridged the Old and New Testaments. His mother, Elizabeth, was a cousin of Jesus' mother, Mary. He was six months older than Jesus. John spent most of his life at home in the hill country of Judea, not far from Jerusalem. His relatively brief public life consisted of preaching in the Jordan River Valley. Urging repentance, he predicted and prepared for the coming of Jesus. John called Jesus "the one greater than myself." He is called the baptizer because he baptized Jesus and many others. John took a strong moral stand against Herod, the king, when he entered into a second marriage. This public stance eventually led him to a martyr's death. The lives of John and Jesus were very similar. Scripture says they "met each other" before they were born when Mary came to Elizabeth's home. They shared the same mission of preaching God's kingdom and a number of Jesus' apostles had received their formation from John. Jesus called John the greatest of the Old Testament. John said Jesus was the greatest of all times.

JUNE 28. IRENAEUS, BISHOP AND MARTYR
2 Tm 2:22-26

Born in Turkey, about 140, Irenaeus was a vital link in the

development of the apostolic traditions. He continues that direct line of witnesses from the time of Jesus into the third century. Irenaeus was a disciple of Polycarp, who in turn was a disciple of John, who was a disciple of Jesus. He labored in Gaul much of his life and opposed the Montanists. This group believed they were called to restore the Church to its primitive simplicity. They claimed direct inspiration of the Holy Spirit and a unique sharing in the charismatic gifts. Irenaeus also opposed the Gnostics, who considered salvation obtainable by knowledge rather than divine faith. Some writings of Irenaeus are extant. They deal mainly with his confrontations against the Gnostics. His main concern was to faithfully hand down the teachings which came from Jesus. Today, we continue to believe in and build on those same teachings which Irenaeus promoted — Scripture, Eucharist and Creed. The last days of Irenaeus are vague. One tradition says he was martyred.

JUNE 29, PETER and PAUL, APOSTLES
Vigil: Jn 21:15-19; Day: Mt 16:13-19

Peter and Paul are certainly household names in the history of the Church. They transport us back to the exciting first century of Christianity and its fledging early thrusts out into the primitive world. Peter was most likely prepared for his mission by the watchful eye of John the Baptizer. He was personally introduced to Jesus, though, by his brother, Andrew. Jesus fashioned him further into the ministry with both high praises and severe condemnations. Peter found his break with the past to be difficult and long. In the end he gave his full commitment by his death on the cross — just like his Master. Paul came to the Church a bit later and in dramatic fashion. Dedicated to his religious roots, he was a devotee to all that was anti-Christian. Suddenly, he made a complete about-face and all his former hatred was baptized into unbridled love. That divine love and grace filled his life so completely that he never experienced a lack of enthusiastic energy. He, too, gave all to Christ with a martyr's death. The two Apostles often had their differences of opinion, about some questions of religion, but were united in the advancement of Jesus' teachings. They remain two outstanding superstars securely enshrined in the Church's hall of fame.

JULY 3. THOMAS, APOSTLE
Ep 2:19-22 and Jn 20:24-29

Most of what we know of the Apostle Thomas comes to us through the Gospel of John. We especially note three incidences where Thomas speaks out and, thereby, gives us an insight into his feelings: (1) When Jesus and his apostles were going to Bethany following the death of Lazarus, Thomas said, "Let us go along to die with him" (Jn 11:16); (2) When Jesus spoke of leaving this world, he told his apostles they knew the way where he was going. Thomas replied, "We do not know where you are going. How can we know the way?" His question evoked that wonderful response: "I am the way, the truth and the life" (Jn 14:4-6); (3) After the resurrection, it was Thomas who wanted more proof of identity of the Risen Lord. His satisfied curiosity gave birth to the classic response, "My Lord and my God" (Jn 20:28). Thomas wanted to know and his questions give us renewed faith. He should not be considered a doubting person, but one who is independent, inquisitive, courageous and saintly. The faith of Thomas and his continual search for deeper understanding has truly enriched us all.

JULY 4. INDEPENDENCE DAY

One of the most popular dates on the American calendar is July 4th. Second only to December 25, it, too, is a birthday celebration. On this day in 1776 our nation was officially born. Birthdays, in general, are happy occasions and the birthday of our beloved country is especially a time of national rejoicing. Philadelphia was the site of our nation's birth. It was that historic city which first witnessed the formal break from the British. President John Adams spoke in a prophetic manner about the future of the Fourth. He said, "It ought to be solemnized with pomp and parade, with shows, games, sports, guns, bells and bonfires from one end of the continent to the other." Although "The Fourth" has been long celebrated, it was not declared a holiday until 1941. This birth certificate of our country promises continuation of life, liberty and the pursuit of happiness. These deep truths, Jefferson said, are both sacred and self-evident. They have become part of the very fabric of our way of life. July 4th is further hallowed by the deaths of John Adams, Thomas Jefferson and James Monroe. Adams and Jefferson died the same day in 1826 — on the fiftieth birthday of our nation. Monroe died five years later. John Adams reminds us of another duty on the Fourth of July. He emphasized that, on this day, we should "give solemn worship and devotion to God Almighty."

JULY 11, BENEDICT, ABBOT
Pr 2:1-9

A religious pilgrimage to Rome and vicinity is not complete without a visit to the abbeys of Subiaco and Monte Cassino. Both were founded by Benedict. He is the author of the most famous and enduring monastic rule ever written. His spiritual influence spans far beyond national boundaries. It has dominated Europe and circled the world. His influence in the life of the Church has been truly legendary. He extended to the West what Anthony of Egypt had begun in the East some years previously. Benedict envisioned the monastery as taking the place of the family in behalf of the monk. This Order brought Christianity and civilization to Western Europe. It, also, is credited with preserving the Christian traditions through the Middle Ages. Inspired by their founder, the Benedictines have always been known for piety, liturgical celebrations and love of learning. Born in 480 A.D., Benedict had sixty-three profitable years of life. His rule still guides millions. He tells us to establish a rhythm for our life in a threefold manner. Allow adequate time for work, recreation, and prayer. In such a way, says Benedict, you will use your time to the very best advantage.

JULY 15. BONAVENTURE. BISHOP AND DOCTOR

Bonaventure is remembered as a brilliant theologian, keen philosopher and Minister General of the Franciscan Order. It was Bonaventure who applied, in a very practical manner, the teachings of Francis of Assisi to the Franciscan Order. Born in 1221, Bonaventure was five years old when Francis died. Bonaventure's world revolved around the teachings of Scripture and the application of these truths to peoples' lives. He was a close personal friend of Thomas Aquinas since the days they taught together at the University of Paris. The love and devotion he felt for Francis of Assisi was also immense. He credits Francis with saving his life, when as a young man, he had been deathly ill. In his teachings on Christology, Bonaventure developed the human nature of Jesus and tried to delve into the Savior's inner life. He also emphasized the significant role of Mary in the devotional life of a Christian. This 13th century Franciscan cardinal was called by Pope Leo XIII, "the prince par excellence who leads us by the hand of God."

JULY 22. MARY MAGDALENE
Sg 3:1-4 or 2 Cor 5:14-17 and Jn 20:1-2, 11-18

We often remember the names of people who were the first to hold a particular office or the first to accomplish some deed. There's the first president, first pope, first person on the moon, etc. Today, the Church celebrates the life of the lady who was the first to see Jesus following his resurrection from the dead. She is Mary of Magdala, a longtime friend of Jesus, who was blessed by him early in his career. In gratitude, Mary followed Jesus with other women and provided for the material needs of Jesus and the apostles. She bravely stood on Calvary during the crucifixion and came to anoint his lifeless body in the tomb. Unexpectedly finding him alive, she uttered those memorable words, "I've seen the Lord." We carry that thought with us today and see the Lord in all the sights, sounds, and people we will meet. We can see the Lord in our pain and in our joy. We, too, can laugh at Cana and cry at Calvary in unison with Jesus. Like Mary of Magdala, we all must learn to seek Jesus, not among the dead, but among the living.

JULY 25. JAMES, APOSTLE
2 Cor 4:7-15 and Mt 20:20-28

James is a blessed and privileged name. It begins and ends with the same letters as the name Jesus and also has the same number of letters. Two of the apostles had the name of James. Scripture distinguishes them by their fathers — James, son of Zebedee and James, son of Alpheus. We celebrated the feast of the son of Alpheus, also called "The Lesser," on May 3. Today we honor, "The Greater," the son of Zebedee. James, "The Greater," was the brother of John. Along with Peter and his younger brother, James was one of the three apostles who viewed some major events which the other nine did not see. Jesus invited these three only to the Transfiguration on Mt. Tabor. In the Garden of Gethsemane, only Peter, James and John were allowed to see the blood and tears of an emotionally wounded Savior. These close encounters with the deepest internal feelings of Jesus altered forever the life of James. Already in the leading group of apostles, he now stepped ahead of even Peter and John by becoming the first apostle to die a martyr's death, in 44 A.D. It was expected, for he had previously told Jesus he was willing to drink the bitter cup.

JULY 26, JOACHIM and ANNE, PARENTS OF MARY
Si 44:1, 10-15 and Mt 13:16-17

Some of the most loving and delightful people we've ever known are our grandparents. In order to give assurance that all children receive the love and influence which only grandparents can give, we are provided with four of them. The Bible doesn't mention the grandparents of Jesus, but tradition says his maternal grandparents were Joachim and Anne. Joseph's father was Jacob according to Matthew, or Heli according to Luke. His mother is not mentioned. Today, Joachim and Anne are honored as saints. That's not surprising, for we think our own grandparents are saints, and all the more those of Jesus. Jesus, as a young boy, most likely spent many days and nights with them. We know they would have been typically proud of their young, energetic grandson. This day, we should show appreciation to our grandparents and all our ancestors. If we enjoy good health, material blessings, and family dignity, we need to thank those who passed these qualities on to us. If we are grandparents, we can pause to think of our dignity as it exists in the minds of our grandchildren.

JULY 29. MARTHA
Jn 11:19-27 or Lk 10:38-42

The name Martha is from the Hebrew "Marta," meaning lady. The famous Martha of the Bible is normally mentioned in conjunction with her sister, Mary, and brother, Lazarus. Luke says it was to their home in Bethany that Jesus went to "take a break" from the ministry. John tells us that Jesus returned to Bethany to raise Lazarus from the dead. On these occasions, we meet Martha and hear her words to Jesus. On the visit when she was left to serve and Mary sat at his feet, Martha was correct in complaining. She was reflecting her Jewish upbringing that the women should serve and not sit and talk. Jesus does not disapprove of Martha's work, but rather praises Mary for moving beyond the old tradition and accepting Jesus as the new teacher. When he returned later to raise Lazarus from the dead, he spoke of new life. Martha replied that she believed in the resurrection on the last day. This shows her developing Christian faith since many Jews did not accept the resurrection. Today, the little town where she lived is still very busy — with tourists. The spirit of Martha lives on.

JULY 31. ST. IGNATIUS OF LOYOLA, PRIEST
1 Cor 10:31 - 11:1

In 1492 Columbus, commissioned by King Ferdinand and Queen Isabella of Spain, discovered America. At that very time, Ignatius was born in Loyola, Spain. He became a knight in the court of this same King and Queen. Like most young men, Ignatius was energetic and anxious to prove himself in battle. So it happened that fighting under the Spanish flag, he was wounded in combat against the French. He was carried into the hospital with one wound and walked out with two healings. Ignatius had been cured in both body and soul. Soon he abandoned the military to establish a spiritual way of life based on some of his military training. He became the founder and leader of the Society of Jesus and made himself and his followers available to the Holy Father, to go anywhere and do whatever work he desired. Now, it was not for the glory of Ignatius or Spain, but for the glory of God. His motto: *Ad Majorem Dei Gloriam* (AMDG) — all for the greater glory of God — became the battle cry of his life. It is said that someone asked Ignatius what he would do if the Holy Father asked him to disband the Jesuits. Would he comply? Ignatius said: "Give me fifteen minutes, then I would do it." His spirit still lives and thrives, not only in the Society he founded, but in millions of Christians which the spirituality of Ignatius has touched and guided.

AUGUST 1. ALPHONSUS LIGUORI, BISHOP AND DOCTOR
Rm 8:1-4

The ninety-one years of Alphonsus Liguori's life spanned almost all of the eighteenth century. This saintly, practical and morally-conscious man was born near Naples, Italy in 1696. Very early in his life it became apparent that he had an extremely acute intellect. The University of Naples opened its doors to him at the age of twelve. Four years later Alphonsus graduated with a doctorate in jurisprudence. After practicing law for eleven years, Alphonsus became disillusioned with his profession and left behind the law courts in order to pursue theology. His studies led him into the priesthood where he was ordained at the age of thirty. Later Alphonsus founded the Congregation of the Most Holy Redeemer (C.SS.R.), better known as the Redemptorists, and eventually became a bishop. He was a tireless writer, producing nearly 120 works on a variety of subjects. He wrote of priestly perfection, pastoral work and techniques of preaching. His sermons were powerful and were later highly admired by another outstanding preacher, Cardinal John Henry Newman. Alphonsus excelled in numerous other spiritual subjects, in moral theology, and in practical decision making. He wrote of the glories of the Blessed Virgin Mary and nearly every phase of the spiritual life. Alphonsus promoted a commonsense approach to the spiritual life by avoiding the extremes. We would be well-advised to do the same.

AUGUST 4, JOHN VIANNEY, PRIEST
Mt 9:35 - 10:1

John was only three years old in 1789 when his fellow countrymen held their famous tennis-court meeting which launched the French Revolution. With the nation in turmoil following the beheadings of King Louis XVI and Queen Marie Antoinette, John received only a few months of formal education. The Revolution made it difficult for him to practice religion and he had to make his First Communion in secret. At an early age, John Vianney began his own personal revolution by subduing his self-will and conforming his life completely to Christ. His rigid asceticism led him to live on potatoes and pray long into the night. He began studying for the priesthood privately at first, then with the assistance of a local pastor. The lack of proper schooling and difficulties with Latin caused John to follow a very uneven and rocky road to ordination. In the meantime, the 230 people of the little village of Ars were waiting patiently for the bishop to assign a pastor to their tiny parish. Little did they know how Providence was to provide for them. John would stay with them for forty-two years, change their hearts, and bring the world to their town. Pope Pius XI would later declare John Vianney the "Patron of all parish priests."

AUGUST 6. TRANSFIGURATION
Dn 7:9-10, 13-14; 2 P 1:16-19 and Mt 17:1-9 or Mk 9:2-10 or Lk 9:28-36

They say that one must visit Mt. Tabor on a bright, warm morning in spring. The clean mountain air mingles with the golden rays of the sun and the soft melodies of the song birds create an atmosphere which is nothing less than ethereal. This picture of peace is highlighted by the memory of Jesus and three of his apostles who one day stood on this same mountain and experienced the glory of God. Moses and Elijah were also present and the voice of God the Father echoed through the trees on that momentous occasion. What a unique spot for the rendezvous of memories. The mountain continues to transfigure those pilgrims who come to pause and pray, as it did Jesus long ago. The miracle of the transfiguration was not that the glory of Jesus was made manifest on that occasion. By nature, Jesus was filled with an inner beauty and glory which normally would shine through all he did and said. The miracle is that the Lord kept his inner glory hidden at other times. Here, he relaxed and it all burst forth as a glorious morning sunrise. Our spiritual journey leads us on to become something we've never been. For us, transfiguration is a fulfillment, an ultimate goal.

AUGUST 8. DOMINIC, PRIEST

The needs of his time called Dominic to his life's mission. One of his major projects was to combat the Albigensians. The devotees of this sect were especially strong in northern Italy and southern France. They taught that the devil is the creator of matter and a rival god. The Christian God created the spirit only — no matter. Anything made up of matter was evil. Salvation is achieved by freeing oneself from all matter. Dominic saw the need to go forth and confront these false teachings which were being promulgated in the name of Christianity. He, consequently, established the Order of Preachers, better known as the Dominicans, to face the opposition. History has recorded their confrontations and some fourteenth-century art shows the Dominicans engaged in debate with the Albigensians. Dominic also devoted his own time and energy to the cause of preaching. This thirteenth-century saint was guided by truth, quick to understand situations, seasoned in his reflections and devoted to prayer. Exhausted by his labors, Dominic died at the age of fifty-one. His energetic spirit, though, continues to be seen today in all who love Jesus and, especially, those who wear that familiar white and black religious habit.

AUGUST 10. LAWRENCE, DEACON AND MARTYR
2 Cor 9:6-10 and Jn 12:24-26

During the years 253-260, the Roman Emperor, Valerian, was in power. In the early part of his reign he showed tolerance to the Christians, but as he suffered military defeats, he demanded that the Christians, too, observe the state religion. Perhaps, he was blaming them for his military failures. In 258, Valerian decreed that "bishops, priests and deacons should be executed immediately . . ." It was at this time that the young Roman deacon, Lawrence, was observed practicing his Christian faith. The oppressive decree of the emperor was brought to bear and Lawrence was led to a martyr's death. Most remember him for the quip made to his torturers about turning him over as he endured death on the gridiron. This and some other details of his death may have been generated more from legend than fact. Some scholars discredit the gridiron story and say he died by the sword. There is common agreement that he died in 258 under Valerian. A church was built over the tomb of Lawrence, which became a very popular place of worship for those making a pilgrimage of faith.

AUGUST 11. CLARE, VIRGIN

It must have been an impressive scene at the site of the Portiunculo in the spring of 1212. There, in his rustic quarters on the plains below Assisi, the thirty-three year old charismatic, Francis, conferred the habit on the beautiful eighteen year old, Clare. Both had forsaken their material inheritances to seek the riches of the spirit. She would give life to the feminine branch of the newly formed Franciscan Order and serve as abbess of the Poor Clare Sisters. She continued in this position all her life, which extended twenty-seven years beyond the death of Francis. Although, Clare suffered from severe illnesses, she is reported to have been a most joyful person which attracted three of her blood sisters and even her mother to join the Poor Clares. Canonization was conferred upon her only two years following her death. Today, a large church is dedicated to her honor in Assisi and her model of the simple life is imitated around the world. More than 800 years have passed since then, but millions continue to visit the mountain town where Francis and Clare still live on in spirit.

AUGUST 14. MAXIMILIAN KOLBE, PRIEST AND MARTYR

The liturgy today rivets our attention on the small town of Oswiecim, in southern Poland, about 35 miles west of Cracow. That was the site of one of the Nazi concentration camps which the world knows as Auschwitz. It was there, in 1941 that a forty-seven year old Catholic priest from Lotz, Poland, 120 miles north, was held captive by the German Gestapo. His name is now very familiar to everyone — Maximilian Kolbe. In retaliation for a prisoner escaping, the Nazis arbitrarily condemned to death Francizek Gajowniczek. When Francizek lamented he would never again see his wife and family, Fr. Kolbe volunteered to die in his place. About two weeks later he was killed. Considered a martyr for his faith, Kolbe was canonized in 1982 by a fellow Polish countryman, Pope John Paul II. The piazza of St. Peter's echoed with the pope's voice quoting the words of Jesus about true love and giving your life for your friends. Among those present in the crowd of 150,000 was Francizek Gajowniczek. He said, "I was never able to thank him personally, but we looked into each others eyes before he was led away."

AUGUST 20. BERNARD, ABBOT AND DOCTOR

It is public record that Bernard and his five brothers and sister inherited a noble ancestry from both their parents. Born near Dijon, in central France, Bernard was the third in the family. His mother, to whom he was very close, died when he was seventeen. Then four years later, in the historic year of 1111, Bernard "left the world" to join the Cistercians, the strictest Order in existence. All his brothers accompanied him. Three years later he was chosen as abbot to begin a new monastery. He and twelve companions selected a peaceful valley which they called Clairvaux. Newly ordained and first-time abbot, twenty-five year old Bernard of Clairvaux began to exercise a tremendous influence on Western Europe. Before his death, sixty-eight new monasteries were begun from Clairvaux. This zealous Abbot of Clairvaux was outspoken in a number of areas. He publicly criticized the famous Benedictine monastery of Cluny for failing to uphold its previously high disciplinary standards. He openly opposed the teachings of the popular Abelard. Bernard preached in support of the Second Crusade, which failed. His writing, preaching, explanation of doctrine, and personal love of Jesus influenced others immensely. Bernard's fifty-two years of earthly life inspired his contemporaries and has left a lasting impression on following generations.

AUGUST 21. PIUS X. POPE

The American author, Horatio Alger, is remembered for his famous series of books for boys. His heroes always rose from poverty and defeat to riches and success. Alger never wrote the life of Joseph Sarto, although he was his contemporary and Sarto's life would have provided excellent material. Joseph (Giuseppe) Sarto, born in northern Italy, was known as a poor boy. One author tells of him carrying his shoes to and from school so that he could preserve them longer. Ordained in 1858, he spent seventeen years in parish life as an associate and pastor. Each of his next assignments ran from eight to ten years — chancellor of the diocese, bishop of Mantua, Cardinal of Venice and Pope of the Universal Church. He is remembered for his motto, "to restore all things in Christ, in order that Christ may be all and in all." We have Pius X to thank for our reception of Holy Communion at the age of seven. If our liturgical music is inspiring today, we should thank Pius X. His spirit of poverty, zeal, faith and devoted love has long outlived him. In 1954, Joseph Sarto was declared a saint.

AUGUST 22. QUEENSHIP OF MARY

Scripture often praises those people who fear the Lord. Mary is one of them. The word "fear" is not to be interpreted as fright or trembling, but reverence. Blessed are those who show reverence and respect to God. Those, who think in lowly ways and do simple and ordinary deeds, are seen as good candidates for superior positions. That is the road Mary followed to her elevated position of Queenship. Mary, as Queen of heaven and earth, is upheld, today, for our admiration and imitation. We try to offer our liturgical worship to God with holy respect and humility as Mary did. To the degree we excel in these basic virtues, to that

degree we imitate the dignity of the Queen. In the Book of
Jeremiah there is a reference to a pagan goddess who is given the
title of queen of heaven. The people light fires and offer cakes to
the queen for protection (Jr 7:18; 44:17-19, 25). They feel these
sacrifices will protect them from harm. Scholars say this queen is
the pagan goddess, Ishtar, whose cult was popular in Judah during
the seventh century B.C. In Christian cultures there is only one
who merits that exalted title. Mary, Queen of Heaven, pray for
us.

AUGUST 24. BARTHOLOMEW. APOSTLE
Rv 21:9-14 and Jn 1:45-51

   Listing the names of the Twelve Apostles can be confusing.
Some share the same name and others have dual names. The two
Jameses must be distinguished as Greater and Less. Two have
the name Simon and one is often called Peter. Matthew is the
same person as Levi. Today's Gospel tells of Nathanael's call, but
he's usually known as Bartholomew. In John's Gospel, he is
always called Nathanael. The others use the name Bartholomew.
The Gospel portrays Nathanael Bartholomew as a happy individual who always tried to see the brighter side of things. He was
very impressed that Jesus knew him before they met. In him, the
Lord said, "there is no guile." He was quick to join Peter to go
fishing after the Resurrection. When Philip told Nathanael that
they had found the Messiah, Jesus of Nazareth, Nathanael jok-
ingly quipped, "Can anything good come out of Nazareth?" He
was reflecting the unsavory reputation of ancient Nazareth.
Nathanael was obviously very impressed by Jesus for, after only a
few minutes and a few words, he felt moved to declare, "You are
the Son of God, you are the King of Israel." Quickly he learned
something good could come out of Nazareth.

AUGUST 27. MONICA
Lk 7:11-17

Monica was born in 331 in the northwest corner of the continent of Africa in the ancient country of Numidia. The former boundaries of Numidia are similar to those of modern Algeria. There, also, was her oldest son, Augustine, born twenty-three years later. Most of the preserved details of her life touch upon her prayer and patient suffering for members of her family. We are not informed how she personally acquired her deep faith and spirituality, but we are told that she tried to convey her convictions to those she loved. Her husband is said to have been irresponsible and caused her a lot of trouble as, also, did her mother-in-law. Her prayers and efforts brought about the reform of both and their acceptance of the Christian religion. Her son Augustine followed, to some extent, the dissolute lifestyle of his father, but the prayers of his mother eventually touched his heart and caused him to reform his life. Monica died at the age of fifty-six and, to this day, is considered the model of all those who hope and pray for the conversion of others.

AUGUST 28. AUGUSTINE, BISHOP AND DOCTOR
1 Jn 4:7-16 and Mt 23:8-12

One of the truly outstanding saints of all times is Augustine. His life bridged the fourth and fifth centuries and his thoughts and influence have bridged every century since. He was born in northwest Africa, in modern day Algeria. Raised in a Christian atmosphere, but not baptized, Augustine, at age sixteen, began to pursue life on the "wild side." For further studies, he went to Carthage, which is the modern day city of Tunis in Tunisia. Later he crossed the Mediterranean to Rome and, then, to Milan where he met Bishop Ambrose, whose influence changed Augustine's life. On the vigil of Easter, Augustine was baptized in Milan, along with his son Adeodatus, whom he had fathered during college days in Carthage. Back home in Algeria (then called Numidia), he was ordained and, eventually, made bishop of Hippo (modern Annaba), where he served for thirty-five years. His theological thoughts and writings are monumental. Two of his more popular works are *Confessions* (about his early life and conversion), and *The City of God* (a defense of Christianity). Two of his most remembered quotes are: "Late have I loved you, O beauty, so ancient yet so new" and "Our hearts were made for you (God) and they shall not rest until they rest in you."

AUGUST 29. BEHEADING OF JOHN THE BAPTIST. MARTYR
Jr 1:17-19 and Mk 6:17-29

Today we recall the gruesome and senseless death of John the Baptizer. We have met him on many pages of the Bible and he seems to be our longtime friend. We've read of his miraculous conception in the womb of his mother, Elizabeth, and heard his desert preaching during Advent. We've witnessed him baptizing Jesus in the Jordan, sending his own disciples to the Lord and telling it "like it is" to common people and royalty alike. It was his condemnation of the divorces and second marriages of the royalty that led to his death. John had a word for every circumstance and occasion but we don't know what he said when told he was about to die. Perhaps he had some words about the drunken, superficial and worldly Herod and his equally dissolute wife, Herodias. However, in that regard, the Bible remains silent. We do know John was ready to die for he, like Simeon of the preceding generation, had run his course, completed his work, seen the Messiah, and knew it was time to fade into the background. Jesus and his disciples were very much disturbed by John's martyrdom. They had to take a break in their ministry. Jesus reminded them there was none better than John the Baptizer.

SEPTEMBER 3. GREGORY THE GREAT, POPE AND DOCTOR

Sylvia and Gordian lived in Rome and had a baby boy, Gregory, born in 540 A.D. Their family had recently given two popes to the Church and, in fifty years, their son also would hold that office. He would be very successful in his personal spiritual life and be canonized a saint. In his papal duties, he would excel to the point that history would attach to his name the title of "Great." Today, we honor the memory of pope St. Gregory the Great. Gregory was blessed with an excellent education, which prepared him for a civil service career. Soon he became the prefect (or mayor) of Rome with the responsibility for presiding over the Roman Senate, the finances, food, defense and policing of the city. Following the death of his father, Gregory completely abandoned civil service and became a monk. In the spiritual life, he excelled with even more fervor than he had when in civil service. His fantastic business ability coupled with his deep spirituality, caused Church leaders to call him from his desired contemplative life into influential religious positions. His contemplative spirituality accompanied him to the papacy and guided him through the fourteen years he spent in that exalted office.

SEPTEMBER (FIRST MONDAY) LABOR DAY

All of nature is at work in some way. The trees produce their fruit, nuts, or grow into use for lumber. The plants, too, are busily shaping their produce. Animals and birds build their shelters and nests where they can feed their young. Bees accomplish much more than we realize for our benefit, and the ants especially have the reputation of being workaholics. Today, we honor human workers and all that they accomplish. Whether our labors are manual, mental, technical, professional, skilled or unskilled, whatever we do gives us dignity and provides us with our livelihood. The ancient directive is to "have dominion over the earth" (Gn). The land is our gift to preserve, dig, build, reshape and form. We engage in a dignified spiritual labor when we come to worship. Here, we honor God as Creator and renew our appreciation to our fellow human beings and all creation which serves us all so well. We are encouraged to give at least a tenth of our labors back to society, as a thanksgiving offering. The old spiritual, *When the Roll is Called Up Yonder*, says: "Let us labor for the Master, from the dawn to setting sun, Let us talk about his wondrous love and care. Then, when, all of life is over and our work on earth is done, When they call the roll up yonder, I'll be there."

SEPTEMBER 8. BIRTH OF MARY
Mi 5:1-4 or Rm 8:28-30 and Mt 1:1-16, 18-23

Mary's prayer is not the Hail Mary, but the Magnificat. The Hail Mary is said about Mary and offered asking for her intercession. The Magnificat contains the words which were conceived in her very heart and expressed by her lips. It's her personal and spontaneous prayer to God. Through the ages, many people have claimed to have seen Mary in some type of vision. Many of her apparitions are doubtful, but she truly makes her first appearance in Scripture in Luke 1:28. There, she is a young virgin, beautiful (full of grace), and engaged to be married. She is speaking with an angel and a bit nervous, for the angel reassures her that she need not be afraid. This is her official, documented debut. We are not told of her actual birth, nor are her parents mentioned in the Bible. Tradition calls them Joachim and Anne. We don't know if she had brothers or sisters. The ancients put much trust in the signs of the zodiac as some do today. Mary is a Virgo. That's a very fitting sign. Her birth, full of grace and free from sin, is a sign that the Messiah will soon be born into the world.

SEPTEMBER 9. PETER CLAVER, RELIGIOUS

Known as the "saint of the slaves," this Jesuit missionary was born in Spain in 1580. At the age of twenty-two, Peter Claver joined the Society of Jesus with the desire to work in the New World. Eight years later found him in Cartagena, Columbia, assisting the African slaves. He saw first-hand the brutal treatment of these kidnapped men and women and it left a deep impression in his soul. From then on, Peter Claver knew his true calling. Later, after being ordained in Bogota, Peter Claver returned to Cartagena for his life's work. He had the distinction of being the first ordained Jesuit priest whose other credentials — he was a doctor and a teacher — were invaluable blessings for his unique ministry. It is said that Peter Claver met the slave ships as they arrived from Africa and immediately boarded those vessels to bring consolation to the captured slaves. Often, they were chained in the holds of the ship, terrified and suffering from disease and despair. His ministry was first medical, then psychological and, eventually, spiritual. He, often, carried them to shore on his own shoulders. It is estimated he baptized over 300,000 slaves and tried to help them regain and maintain a sense of self-worth.

SEPTEMBER 13. JOHN CHRYSOSTOM, BISHOP AND DOCTOR

A baby boy born at the midpoint of the fourth century (349 A.D.) was named in honor of the Apostle John. Later, in the sixth century, the world would call him Chrysostom, as a tribute to his "golden mouth." Religious division and an exhilarating culture thrived side by side in John's home town of Antioch as he grew to manhood. His Greek mother, widowed at the age of twenty, meticulously directed his education. John, through birth and learning, possessed the best of the Roman and Greek refinements. Desiring the life of a monk, he lived with spiritual directors and, then, two years alone in a cave. Ordained at the age of thirty-six, he ministered in Antioch where he became noted for his superb eloquence. Within twelve years, he received the prestigious office of bishop of Constantinople. Many reforms were awaiting the arrival of Chrysostom and to each he gave his energetic attention. He abruptly stopped the wasting of Church money, built hospitals for the poor, ousted wayward deacons, disciplined the clergy and ordered the monks to their monasteries. He also deposed six bishops for simony. John was fearless, blunt, talented, saintly and very fascinating.

SEPTEMBER 14. TRIUMPH OF THE CROSS
Nb 21:4-9; Ph 2:6-11 and Jn 3:13-17

The most widely recognized sign of Christianity is the cross. It is to the Church what the flag is to the country. It is with this sign that we bless ourselves, others and various objects. Once the cross was one of the world's most hated signs, similar to the electric chair, gas chamber, guillotine, firing squad or hanging rope. Death, by crucifixion, was regarded as the most cruel form of capital punishment. Cicero, the Roman Senator, said no cross should ever come near a Roman soldier. What originally was a sign of punishment and death, now symbolizes abundant life. Our Mass today has as its theme the Triumph of the Cross. When the early Christians first began to honor the cross because of its close association to Jesus, the non-Christians rebelled. St. Paul called it an obstacle to the Jews and madness to the Greeks and Romans. Death by crucifixion was officially terminated about 350 A.D., but the crosses have continued to multiply. It is still a sign of pain, but the pain it represents is the price of victory and salvation.

SEPTEMBER 15. OUR LADY OF SORROWS
Heb 5:7-9 and Jn 19:25-27 or Lk 2:33-35

Today, we might like to remain standing during the homily to commemorate Mary's most pain-filled day. The first line of the Gospel speaks a deep and meditative truth. It reminds us of the hymn we often sing at the stations: "By the cross her station keeping, stood the mournful mother weeping, close to Jesus to the last." Standing is the position of readiness for whatever may happen. On Calvary, Mary was on her feet ready to assist Jesus if she could in any way. When the TV program loses the picture, a voice tells us to "stand by." There is a popular song with lyrics to "stand by your man." It was at his painful scene of death that Mary stood by her man, her son and her God. We know of the natural sorrow which exists at any death scene, especially between a mother and her child. We know that a mother nearby would experience every pain and hurt and wish that she could suffer in place of her child. These would be the same thoughts that flowed through the sensitive soul of Mary. Like Mary, do we stand by others when they are in sorrow and need? Do we stand up for what we believe? Mary stands for Jesus. For what do we stand?

SEPTEMBER 16. CORNELIUS. POPE AND MARTYR and
CYPRIAN. BISHOP AND MARTYR

Cornelius, a pope, and Cyprian, a bishop, share this feastday as they shared many days in the ministry of the early Church. When Pope Fabian died in 250, Emperor Decius was persecuting the Christians in Rome, which delayed the papal election. The Church was governed by a group of priests for about a year until Decius left town on a military expedition. Cornelius, then, was elected pope. Novatian, who had been one of the governing priests, protested and had himself declared as pope. Some bishops supported him, but one who did not was Cyprian, the bishop of Carthage. He rallied in behalf of Pope Cornelius, who prevailed. That same year, 251, Novatian and his followers opposed Cornelius for accepting public sinners back into the Church. Again, Cyprian supported the pope and condemned the Novatianists. Persecution by the Roman Emperor was resumed the following year. Bombarded from within by Novatian and from without by Decius, Cornelius died after a brief and turbulent two-year reign. Liturgically, Cyprian continues to stand by the pope.

SEPTEMBER 21. MATTHEW, APOSTLE AND EVANGELIST
Ep 4:1-7, 11-13 and Mt 9:9-13

Jesus spoke two simple words and Matthew's life was never the same again. "Follow me," the Lord said, and Matthew did just that. He did not ask when, where, or how much do you pay. He simply began to follow Jesus. Matthew makes a complete about-face. He left a secure job with the state to work for the Church. He went from a tax-collecting position to a tax-exempt organization. His lifestyle changed from sitting at a desk receiving peoples' payments to giving out salvation messages on the road. Matthew threw a party at his home for his former friends at the internal revenue office as a formal good-bye. Jesus was invited to the party. The house and party show Matthew to be a man of some wealth. His job in the revenue department probably required some education. His background was different from the majority of the Apostles who had been fishermen. In his Gospel, Matthew calls himself by his proper name, but Mark and Luke refer to him as Levi. Little is known of his life following his call, but he will live on through his Gospel. It is used in our liturgy more than any of the others.

SEPTEMBER 27, VINCENT DE PAUL, PRIEST

If a person is hungry, in need of clothes or a place of shelter for the night, help can often be found at the local St. Vincent de Paul Society. Members of this charitable institution are found in most cities and in many countries. This society takes its name and inspiration from the saint whom we honor at this liturgy. Vincent was born in Pouy, France in 1581. The name of the city has since been changed to St. Vincent de Paul. He was the third of six children of a peasant family. He was ordained to the priesthood and gradually saw his life being shaped to helping the poor. Inspired by his friends, Francis de Sales and Jane Frances de Chantal, who both became future saints, Vincent continued in this social ministry. He founded the missionary congregation of the Vincentians and the Sisters of Charity. After a lifetime of trying to fulfill the command of Jesus to "love one another," Vincent died in 1660 and was canonized a saint in 1885. He has been designated as the patron of charitable institutions. What he established in the seventeenth century, is still giving help and hope to the poor of today.

SEPTEMBER 29, MICHAEL, GABRIEL, and RAPHAEL, ARCHANGELS
Dn 7:9-10, 13-14 or Rv 12:7-12 and Jn 1:47-51

Our movies and TV fantasy flicks keep alive the theory that intelligent beings inhabit outer space. They are generally portrayed as creatures who travel with staggering speed, have a technology far more advanced than ours, and who appear much differently than we do physically. Considering the vastness of the physical universe, the existence of this type of intelligent life seems a distinct possibility. Our faith agrees with this kind of speculation when it speaks of the kingdom of God and refers to at least some of the intelligent creatures which inhabit it as angels.

The Bible, in both the Old and New Testaments, has numerous references to these mysterious spiritual creatures. In fact, the Church has an entire theological treatment of them under the heading of "Angelology." It is a dogma that, besides the visible world, God also created a kingdom of invisible spirits called angels (Lateran Council IV). Some were malevolent, as Lucifer, while others were benevolent, as those named in today's liturgy. The biblical names of the angels whose feast we are celebrating are Michael, the warrior; Gabriel, the messenger; and Raphael, the companion. They are called the servants of the King of the universe. We cannot know all the varieties of life which populate this mysterious universe, but these we call our friends.

SEPTEMBER 30. JEROME, PRIEST AND DOCTOR
2 Tm 3:14-17

Jerome was born in northern Italy in 345 A.D. and was twelve years old when he came to Rome to study. After being baptized at the age of nineteen, he travelled through Europe and the Middle East. He then spent two solitary years in the desert where he concentrated on the study of Scripture, spirituality and his understanding of Greek and Hebrew. At the age of thirty-seven he returned to Rome and, for a time, served as the Pope's private secretary. Through his ongoing studies and frequent travels, Jerome became a very knowledgeable person. His views on most subjects were clear and decisive and he was never shy in expressing them. Nor was he hesitant in speaking his mind about the lifestyles of the rich. He would often offend others with his blunt views, but he could equally soothe with his virtue and kindness. Jerome was more given to finding the truth than trying to please people. Many would designate him the most learned person of his time and much of this learning centered about translating and interpreting the Scriptures. His major contribution was his translation of the Bible into the vernacular of the day which was Latin. His love was the Bible and he advised people to read it often. "When your head nods," he said, "it should rest on the sacred page."

OCTOBER 1. THERESE OF THE CHILD JESUS. VIRGIN
Is 66:10-14 and Mt 18:1-4

Therese of Lisieux is the famous French Carmelite sister who became known world-wide for her simple approach to religious life and her priceless autobiography. Born in 1873, she was the youngest of the nine Martin children. Her mother died when she was four and a few years later the family moved to Lisieux, located 100 miles west of Paris. When she was ten, Therese suffered spasms, disorientation and periods of unconsciousness for several months. Then, instantly, she was cured of her strange illness, a cure which she attributed to the Blessed Virgin Mary. Soon she began a time in her life which she called her "conversion." Again, almost instantly, she acquired a remarkable spiritual maturity. Her sister, Celine, verifies both the complete change which took place in her and its dramatic nature. Through persistence, she was able to enter the convent at the age of fifteen. Within ten years, she would die but not before she had completely given her life to God. To the novices, she taught her "Little Way": to do and to suffer even the most inconsequential thing in the most perfect manner possible for the honor and glory of God. From tuberculosis, she suffered more than she thought possible. She died with the words, "My God I love you," on her lips.

OCTOBER 2, GUARDIAN ANGELS
Ex 23:20-23 and Mt 18:1-5, 10

There are well over 300 separate references to angels in the Bible. We find them all the way from Genesis to Revelation. The angels have a variety of duties to perform, but most fulfill their basic function of being messengers, which is the root meaning of the word. The common teaching about angels says they were created before the creation of human beings. They are, likewise considered to be far superior in intelligence than the human species. Therefore, out of concern or pity for us, some angels serve as our guardians. Through the ages, literature, paintings and iconography portray angels in protecting capacities. We are somewhat like their little sisters and brothers, who are younger and less knowledgeable and, thus, in need of a spiritual keeper. It is intriguing that, although Israel did not believe in intermediaries between God and people, their Scriptures are still filled with angels. Jesus emphasizes the role of the protecting angel in Matthew 18:10. He says, "Do not despise one of these little ones, for their angels in heaven always behold the face of my Father in heaven."

OCTOBER 4, FRANCIS OF ASSISI
Gal 6:14-18

Francis is one of those rare saints who has managed to capture the attention and admiration of the entire world. His life and deeds inspire people of all ages and the appeal of this saint cuts across national boundaries and religious differences. Born in 1181, the forty-four years of his life bridge the twelfth and thirteenth centuries. Eight hundred years after his birth, we still, universally, sing his praises. We reflect this day on his profound respect for God and his tender love and attention to all creation.

Many dogs, cats, birds, hamsters, and all kinds of animals will receive a loving pat on the head, a blessing and, perhaps, a choice meal today, compliments of St. Francis. Millions through the years have traveled to his hometown of Assisi, Italy, and visited his private retreat, located high in the Apennine Mountains. From that vantage point, one can obtain a beautiful panoramic view of the valley around Assisi. The life of Francis still challenges us to sort through our lives and discard the useless. He is the example of a peaceful person. His holiness was so evident, Francis was canonized only two years after his death.

OCTOBER 7, OUR LADY OF THE ROSARY

In 1974, Pope Paul VI wrote a papal encyclical about Mary, the Mother of Jesus. The pope made mention of the rosary, saying it is meant to be prayed with a "quiet rhythm and lingering pace." He was emphasizing the fact that this is a meditative prayer and should not be mechanically or hurriedly recited. If we would say, "Let's get in a quick rosary," we would be approaching that prayer in an improper manner. The rosary is a resume of the lives of Jesus and Mary. It leads the person who is praying it through the high and low points of their lives. The joyful mysteries cover a period of thirteen years, the sorrowful have a span of eighteen hours and the glorious extend over a number of years. In praying over these events, we think of our own joys and sorrows and reevaluate them with a more meaningful and spiritual outlook. The rosary is a summary of Christology, Mariology and personal spirituality if we approach it correctly. This feast was instituted in commemoration of the Christian victory over the Turkish fleet in the Gulf of Corinth, off the coast of Greece in 1517. It is commonly known by the Italian name of Lepanto. This was the last major sea battle fought by oar-powered ships.

OCTOBER 15, TERESA OF AVILA, VIRGIN
Rm 8:22-27

Teresa of Avila, born in 1515, is remembered as the famous Spanish Carmelite mystic and reformer. Her mother, Beatriz, married at the age of fifteen, and died when Teresa was fifteen. Feeling very sad and alone, Teresa appealed to the Blessed Virgin to be her mother. Her father, Alonso, then entrusted her to the care of the Augustinian sisters. After a year, she returned home and several years later joined the Carmelites. She became seriously ill, to the point of death, for nearly three years. When she did recover, her legs remained paralyzed for another long period of time. At the age of thirty-nine, she began to experience a strong sense of Christ living within her. Having revitalized herself, she attempted to reform the convent by establishing a more eremitical or secluded style of living. After threats, divisions, and turmoil, she achieved her goal in the establishment of a new foundation. The Order approved and asked her to establish others. She accomplished this and directed the sisters in their return to the original, stricter rule of life. In her work, *The Interior Castle*, she best explains her approach to spirituality. In 1582, Gregory XIII reformed the calendar by dropping ten days. October 4 was followed by October 15. On that historic night, Teresa, the reformer, died.

OCTOBER 17, IGNATIUS OF ANTIOCH, BISHOP AND MARTYR
Ph 3:17 - 4:1 and Jn 12:24-26

Ignatius is remembered as an early bishop of Antioch, Syria, a convert from paganism, and one who truly desired to give his life in martyrdom. He was arrested in Antioch and ordered to be brought to Rome to die. On his way, Ignatius wrote his seven famous letters. These offer both a penetrating view into the depth of his spirituality and clear picture of Church life at the beginning of the second century. He teaches many things about the person of Christ, the virgin birth, Eucharist and the manner in which the Church was actually functioning. The letters also offer thanks to the people in the various cities for their concern for his fate and entrusts them to God's care. He insisted that they do not use political pressure to try to have him set free. He thought of himself as the "wheat of God . . . , to be ground by the teeth of wild beasts, to become the pure bread of Christ." Ignatius met his desired fate in the Coliseum in Rome about the year 110. Ignatius leaves us not only a record of many of the beliefs and teachings of the early Church, but he represents a direct link through Polycarp to the Apostle John. What Ignatius says, therefore, comes directly from the teachings of Jesus.

OCTOBER 18, LUKE, EVANGELIST
2 Tm 4:9-17 and Lk 10:1-9

Luke is a household name. His two major contributions to Scripture make him the most prolific writer of the New Testament. He was born in Syria and was a longtime traveling companion of Paul. He is recognized as a meticulous historian, a medical doctor, and an accomplished author. Were it not for Luke, we would be without the story of the annunciation, visitation, Magnificat, birth of John the Baptizer, and the birth of Jesus. We, also, would be missing many parables such as the lost sheep, lost coin, prodigal son, ten lepers, etc. He was not Jewish and his Gospel clearly shows the work of a Gentile who is writing for a Gentile audience. He writes with more polished Greek than either Matthew or Mark. His Gospel mentions and highlights many of the deeds and sayings of Jesus which shows the Lord's mercy. Two examples are the parable of the publican and sinner and the promise to the thief on the cross. The Acts is absolutely invaluable as the picture of life in the very primitive Christian community. It is often called the "Gospel of the Holy Spirit." It moves geographically from Jerusalem to Rome and then stops. Luke wants everyone to know that Jesus came to bring salvation to all nations.

OCTOBER 19, ISAAC JOGUES and HIS COMPANIONS, MARTYRS

In 1534, St. Ignatius of Loyola, in union with six others, founded the Society of Jesus. A member of that original group was also a future saint — Francis Xavier. The following century, Jesuit missionaries were laboring in North America. They professed and lived the motto of their Society, which had been chosen by the founders, "All for the greater glory of God." Today, we remember and honor a group of eight who died professing that same motto. Commonly known as the North American martyrs, this group of Frenchmen, consisting of six priests and two laymen were martyred over a seven year period (1642-1649). They died both in Canada in the Georgian Bay area and in the vicinity of Albany, N.Y. The name Isaac Jogues normally heads the list. The other Jesuit priests were: John de Brebeuf, Anthony Daniel, Gabriel Lalement, Charles Granier and Noel Chabanel. The martyred lay persons were Rene Goupil, who was a surgeon, and John Lalande. They were ministering to the Hurons and were killed by the Iroquois, after being brutally tortured. Some of the Huron converts were also martyred. All were canonized by Pius XI in 1930.

OCTOBER 28, SIMON and JUDE, APOSTLES
Ep 2:19-22 and Lk 6:12-16

After he had spent an entire night in prayer on a lonely mountain, Jesus chose the twelve Apostles. From a group of disciples numbering at least seventy-two, only twelve were selected. We wonder how the Lord indicated which ones he wanted. Did he call them by name? Perhaps point to them? Maybe he walked through the crowd and laid his hand on the ones he wanted. Do you suppose the other sixty felt relieved or rejected that they were not selected? Simon and Jude were among the chosen Twelve. They became known as the "in between" apostles, being neither leaders nor defectors. Simon is the quiet one. We have no information about him other than the fact that he was on the official list of Apostles. Jude, also called Judas, is sometimes referred to as Thaddaeus. Perhaps he was sometimes confused with the other Judas. John, on one occasion calls him Judas, but quickly adds, "not Judas Iscariot" (Jn 14:22). In the list of the twelve, the name Judas, Son of James, is mentioned only in Luke, in both the Gospel and Acts (Lk 6:16, Ac 1:13); Matthew and Mark use Thaddaeus. This Simon was not Simon Peter. This Judas was not Judas Iscariot. They were common, ordinary, in between people, like ourselves. No doubt that's why Jesus chose them.

NOVEMBER 2. ALL SOULS DAY

In any airport, or bus and train station, we are told two things: the times for arrivals and departures. The vital statistics column in the newspaper informs the public of the new babies who have arrived. The obituary column gives the details of the recent departures. They're usually on the same page. For men and women, like planes and buses, it's a constant coming and going, of births and of deaths, in time's one-way flow. We don't read our own obituary accounts but, if we did, we would, most likely, all confess to much work left undone and, sadly, to many dreams unfulfilled, for it's never really time to die. On All Souls Day, we remember those who have passed from this world and, especially, those we knew and loved. Today we remember them in a less emotional manner than we did on the days they died and were buried. We recall them with deep love and loss, but time has helped to heal the hurt and we can, now, see from a better perspective. It helps us to think ahead to our own eternal departure time as we do for every earthly departure time, for we know that every earthly reality will someday pass. We all owe God one death. God gave one for us; we must give one in return.

NOVEMBER 4. CHARLES BORROMEO, BISHOP

Charles Borromeo was destined from birth to become a leading Church figure. His mother, from the prestigious de Medici family, made sure her son received an excellent education. He was privately tutored in Milan and then studied law at the University of Pavia, where he received a doctorate. When Charles was twenty-one years old, his uncle, Cardinal de Medici, was elected pope and took the name of Pius IV. The pope soon called his nephew to Rome and within a year made him a cardinal. He filled many positions in the Roman Curia, but his most important was in the Secretariat of State during the third period of the Council of Trent. He tirelessly labored to bring the Council reforms into the lives of the clergy and people. One major project was the establishment of seminaries. Later, he became Archbishop of Milan where he exhibited extraordinary pastoral skill. His dedication to Church reform caused opposition from some factions and his life was threatened. Once he was shot while at prayer, but wounded only slightly. Charles Borromeo has had a tremendous impact on Catholic life the last 400 years. He was canonized a saint in 1610.

NOVEMBER 9, DEDICATION OF ST. JOHN LATERAN

Our attention today is drawn to a church building in Rome. It's not the biggest nor most ornate church in the Eternal City, but it is the cathedral church of Rome. The cathedral in a diocese is the church of the bishop where his chair is located. The pope's chair is in St. John Lateran. This cathedral was named after the hill on which it was built. The land for it was donated to the pope by the Emperor Constantine following his conversion to Christianity. No church or public oratory was permitted to be built before this time in the Roman empire. St. John has the unique distinction of being the first publicly consecrated church. That occurred on November 9, 324. It also marked the end of the public persecution of Christians by the state which had previously taken so many lives. The many Christian churches around the world today invite people to come inside to pray and find peace. In our church, as in any basilica or cathedral, we read the same Bible, offer the same worship and serve the same God. Our churches welcome all and call us to unity. Our church buildings provide us with sacred spaces in which to express to God our fears, hurts, hopes and aspirations.

NOVEMBER 10, LEO THE GREAT, POPE AND DOCTOR

We have here a personal close-up of an outstanding leader of the Church. The titles of pope, doctor, and saint grace his name, and history has added another accolade — "The Great." Three popes have been designated as "Great." Leo was the first in 461, then Gregory in 604 and Nicholas in 867. There have been no "great" popes since the year 867. Leo was from Tuscany, in the area of Florence. He worked as a deacon under Pope Celestine in behalf of the poor. Under Pope Sixtus, he accomplished many other missions which often took him out of the country. He was in

Gaul when Pope Sixtus died and he was elected pope. He showed a tremendous respect for the papal office and often said that St. Peter functioned in the person of the pope. In 451, he called the Council of Chalcedon which defined the two natures in Christ. Leo has the reputation of being as feisty as those who tried to subdue him. One tradition says he physically blocked Attila the Hun from entering Rome. The people said, "Peter has spoken through Leo." Many of his doctrinal teachings are very modern. He especially emphasized the indwelling of the Holy Spirit and the presence of the Lord in our daily lives. Leo is a clear window into the fifth century Church and a continual inspiration.

NOVEMBER 11, MARTIN OF TOURS, BISHOP
Mt 25:31-40

The word tour is from the French *"tourner"* meaning to turn. It's often used in military parlance as a "tour of duty." We also tour in the sense of going on a trip. All of these concepts were prevalent in the life of Martin. He was born about 316 in Hungary, of non-Christian parents who soon after traveled to Pavia, Italy, where he was reared. When he was fifteen, he joined the military and served for at least five years. During that time he was baptized. The call of the monastic life attracted his attention and led him to Milan. Eventually, he went to France and, there, established the first French monastery. Later, he was made Bishop of Tours, which is about 125 miles southwest of Paris. He preferred the monastery to the cathedral as his residence, thus living out of the city where he established many rural parishes. He also fought against Arianism which had gained a stronghold in France. He died at the age of eighty-one. Martin's feast is observed on Veterans' Day, which is fitting for a former soldier. The story of sharing his cloak with a beggar may be folklore, but he truly shared God's love with many people, in many ways.

NOVEMBER 12, JOSAPHAT, BISHOP AND MARTYR

Many of the forty-three years of his life were spent by Josaphat working for Christian unity. He is often called the "Apostle of Union." His untimely death, in 1623, was brought about by those who opposed his efforts to bring together the Lithuanian and Ruthenian Christians. Early in his life he was influenced by certain clergy who were adhering to the decision at the Union of Brest. This was an agreement made in 1596 which united the Ruthenian Orthodox with the Roman Catholic Church in Poland. The bond, which was enacted at the city of Brest on the Poland-Russian border, was political in nature as well as religious. Josaphat became a member of the Basilian monastery and was ordained five years later. He used his native energy and speaking ability to foster the cause of unity, and eventually he was made the Archbishop of Pototsk. This gave him a more powerful platform from which to proclaim his message. His opponents accused him of trying to westernize or "Latinize" the Ukrainian Church and that precipitated his martyrdom.

NOVEMBER 13, FRANCES XAVIER CABRINI, VIRGIN

The many books and articles written about Mother Cabrini say she came from Italy to work in the United States. It would be more correct to say that she commuted between Italy and the United States. This tiny lady, who was once refused entrance into the convent because of her frailty, crossed the ocean thirty times. Frances was the last of thirteen children of Agostino and Stella Cabrini of Lombardy, Italy. At eighteen, she took a permanent vow of virginity with the intention of entering the Daughters of the Sacred Heart. Having been weakened by smallpox, she was refused, which led her to the House of Providence Orphanage. Here she took the habit and began her charitable work. Wishing to go to China, but persuaded by others to come to the U.S., she first docked in New York City in 1889 with six religious sisters. Here she began her work with Italian immigrants. In 1909, she became an American citizen. Frances founded numerous convents, schools, orphanages and hospitals in the United States, South America and Europe. She died in Chicago and is buried in New York City, in Mother Cabrini High School. She is the first canonized American saint.

NOVEMBER 17. ELIZABETH OF HUNGARY, RELIGIOUS

The popularity of the name Elizabeth in Hungarian families is traced to a twenty-four year old saint from the thirteenth century. She was born in 1207, the daughter of Catherine and King Andrew II. Although Hungarian by birth, Princess Elizabeth, while still a baby, was affianced to the German Prince, Louis IV. She was raised in Wurtburg Castle in eastern Germany, with all the customs of that country. At the age of fourteen, she married Louis. It was a very happy marriage from which three children were born. Elizabeth zealously devoted herself to caring for the sick and poor. Tragedy invaded her peaceful existence, with the death of her husband, when she was only twenty years old. Her in-laws offered her nothing but cold rejection. Grief-stricken, she and her children left the castle. In her city of refuge, Eisenach, she continued to receive only bitter disdain from others. She joined the Third Order of St. Francis of Assisi and was, at last, able to find some consolation. There, Elizabeth made a concentrated effort to live in the spirit of St. Francis, who was her contemporary. After provisions were made for her children, she gave away her possessions and continued to serve the poor and outcast. She was canonized just four years after her early death.

NOVEMBER 21, PRESENTATION OF MARY

Since we have no historical records of the Blessed Virgin Mary before her teenage years, this celebration today is based on what was customarily done in Jewish tradition. The Mosaic Law said first-born males were to be presented in the temple forty days after their birth. At this time the mother would undergo a purification ceremony (Ex 13:12-16). Following the birth of a girl, the law said a woman was to be in seclusion for eighty days. (So many Old Testament laws, such as this, did a disservice to the equal dignity of women). After her confinement, the mother was to come to the temple to perform her duty of purification as directed in Leviticus (12: 5-8). There is nothing stated that the daughter was to be presented at that time, but only that the mother was to be purified. The custom may have developed of bringing the daughter with her, as was done with the first-born males. Whatever happened in the case of Mary and, whether it occurred when she was eighty days old or not, the fact is that she was dedicated to a lofty ideal. Her entire life was a total presentation to God and her heart always beat to the tune of divine inspiration.

NOVEMBER (FOURTH THURSDAY OF THE MONTH), THANKSGIVING DAY

Thanksgiving Day is meant to be more than a single day on which we express thanks. Originally, of course, it was intended as an occasion to show appreciation for the abundant harvest season. It should extend, though, to more than just a day, a season, or a year. Ideally, we should live in a spirit of continual thanksgiving. It's meant to be the habitual attitude we carry with us for a lifetime. The psalmist says, "I will bless the Lord at *all* times, his praise shall *continually* be in my mouth" (Ps 34:2). We have literally thousands of reasons to be appreciative. Our litanies of thanksgiving would normally include: good health, plenty of food, a fine home, a caring family, loving friends and a strong country. Then, there are all the wonderful freedoms we possess as citizens of the United States. The list is practically unending. How easy it is to take them all for granted and never reflect or recall where our blessings originated. Who died that we would have these many benefits? Who has been especially good to us? Have we, or how have we, said thanks? The Old Testament recommends spending not only a day for celebrating thanksgiving but seven weeks each year. Jesus asks us not only to be thankful but to express our thanks. Could we transform this annual holiday into a personal holyday?

NOVEMBER 30, ANDREW, APOSTLE
Rm 10:9-18 and Mt 4:18-22

The Apostle Andrew was once a fisherman on the Sea of Galilee, along with his brother Peter. It's uncertain if he was a younger or older brother than Peter, but the Bible explicitly says he introduced Peter to Jesus. Andrew is always listed among the four disciples who were closest to Jesus. In his Gospel, John provides a lot of information about Andrew for they were close friends and associates. Both had been apostles of John the Baptizer. The name Andrew means "the brave one." Tradition says that about the year 70 A.D., he very bravely faced crucifixion in Greece on an X-shaped cross. The X-shaped cross today is known as the St. Andrew cross. On this feast day, when we honor and celebrate the life of Andrew, we might try to imitate the virtues of this popular saint. One way would be to introduce someone to Jesus. That could be accomplished by explaining some scriptural truth to one seeking answers in their life. An even more effective way to introduce Jesus to another is by living in such a way that another would be attracted to discover the source of your strength.

DECEMBER 3. FRANCIS XAVIER, PRIEST

The Church has four outstanding saints by the name of Francis (Frances) — three men and one woman. They are all commemorated in the Church calendar. There is Frances Cabrini, teacher and advocate of the poor; Francis de Sales, preacher and writer; and the ever-popular Francis of Assisi. Francis Xavier, the remarkable Jesuit missionary whom we honor today, is the fourth. Francis Xavier was a universal-minded type of man. He was born in Northern Spain in 1506, in the city of Sanguesa about sixty miles south of the French border. Francis continued his studies in Paris at the College of Saint Barbara, where he befriended Pierre Favre and, then, Ignatius Loyola. They were the first three founding members of the future Society of Jesus. Francis and Ignatius were ordained together at Venice four years later. He ministered in Italy, India, the East Indies, Japan, and almost reached China. He died at age forty-six, on a small island not far from Canton. Francis Xavier is the patron saint of the Orient and a truly inspiring model of all dedicated missionaries. He wanted all to hear the hopeful and love-filled message of Jesus.

DECEMBER 7. AMBROSE. BISHOP AND DOCTOR

Ambrose was born in Germany in 339, where his father was serving in a high position for the Roman Empire. After his father's untimely death, Ambrose went to Rome to pursue his studies in law and civil service. At the age of thirty-one, he was promoted to the position of provincial governor of Liguria with his residence in Milan. At that time, the followers of Arius were strong and numerous in northern Italy. When an Arian bishop died, a bitter dispute erupted between the traditional Catholics and the Arians over who would be the next bishop. Ambrose was obliged to restore peace and order. As a result of the way he handled matters, both factions surprisingly came to the unanimous decision that Ambrose should be the new bishop. Within a few days, he was baptized, ordained and made the bishop of Milan. He immediately began his study of theology as he continued to successfully settle the weighty matters of Church and state. He was civilly shrewd and religiously pastoral. Ambrose changed the history of the world when his preaching brought the young African grammar teacher, Augustine, to the baptismal font.

DECEMBER 12, OUR LADY OF GUADALUPE

About 350 miles southwest of Brownsville, Texas is located the city of Guadalupe, Mexico. It is one of the most frequented shrines of Mary in North America. Tradition says it was there on December 9, 1531, one of the native Indians, Juan Diego, saw the Blessed Virgin Mary. Juan was asked by Mary to take her request to the bishop that a church be built on the spot where she was standing. Several days later she again appeared to Juan asking him to pick some flowers for the bishop. He gathered them in his mantle and when he presented them to the bishop, a beautiful image of Mary, as an Indian maiden, was found to be painted on his mantle. Juan Diego's communications with Bishop Zumarraga were through an interpreter, since Juan did not know Spanish and the bishop did not understand the Indian language. The interpreter, Fr. Gonzales, later devoted his life to the evangelization of the Indians. A brand new basilica now stands in the square next to the old one which for centuries commemorated the spot where Mary appeared. The mantle bearing her image is enshrined in a place of honor behind the main altar where pilgrims daily flock to pay homage to the Virgin Mother of all the Americas.

DECEMBER 13, LUCY, VIRGIN AND MARTYR

The facts about the life of Lucy are sketchy. Basically, she is remembered as a martyr who gave her life for the Lord in Syracuse, Sicily in 304 A.D. It was a time when the weakening Roman Empire and the growing Christian Church were facing a showdown. There was but little standing ground between them. People were called to be either Christian or anti-Christian. Lucy represents one of those many saints who dared to clearly state her religious beliefs in the face of violent opposition. The Roman military lieutenant, Galerius, unsheathed his sword with barbaric vengeance at this time in history. In his wake, the blood of Christian martyrs colored every road as dark smoke carried away their possessions. This mighty military thrust against the Church led him to the office of Roman Emperor. On his deathbed, just seven years after the death of Lucy, Galerius agreed to tolerate the Christians and begged their prayers and forgiveness. That same century, in 380, Emperor Theodosius, would make Christianity the official state religion and ban the worship of the old pagan gods. In this final foray of legalized murder, Lucy's name is a lasting reminder of those innocent victims of every age whose blood speaks louder than the sword.

DECEMBER 14, JOHN OF THE CROSS, PRIEST AND DOCTOR

John inherited suffering from his overly class-conscious grandparents. It prepared him for a life of spiritual sorrow which became the hallmark of his success and sanctity. His grandparents, wealthy Spanish silk merchants, disowned his father, Gonzalo, for marrying his mother, Catalina. Since she was only a common silk weaver, she was considered beneath their "class." This ostracism brought severe pain and poverty to their family and led John's father to an early death in 1542. John attended an elementary school for the poor, where he had food and clothing provided. He was drawn to the priesthood and ordained at the age of twenty-five. While offering his first Mass in Medina, he met Teresa of Avila. She spoke to him of reforming the Carmelites to their primitive Rule and solicited his help. John joined the Carmelites, accepted the primitive Rule and changed his name to John of the Cross. John suffered much for the reform of the Order and once was even imprisoned for nine months in a very small cell as his fellow monks tried to make him withdraw his support, but he didn't. There, he wrote some of his most beautiful poetry. His many writings, especially on "The Dark Night of the Soul," explain his mystical search for God. John died on Dec. 13, 1591, speaking the words of the psalmist: "Into your hands, O Lord, I commend my spirit."

978-0-595-36013-0
0-595-36013-0

Printed in the United States
79537LV00002B/1-123